Early Medieval Arabic:

Studies on al-Khalīl ibn Aḥmad

Early Medieval Arabic:
Studies on al-Khalīl ibn Aḥmad

EDITED BY

Karin C. Ryding

GEORGETOWN UNIVERSITY PRESS / WASHINGTON, D.C.

Georgetown University Press, Washington, D.C.

Printed in the United States of America

10 9 8 7 6 5 4 3 2 1 1998

THIS VOLUME IS PRINTED ON ACID-FREE OFFSET BOOK PAPER

Library of Congress Cataloging-in-Publication Data

Early medieval Arabic : studies on al-Khalīl ibn Aḥmad / Karin C. Ryding, editor

p. cm.

Includes bibliographical references.

1. Khalīl ibn Aḥmad, 718?-786?--Contributions in Arabic language.
2. Philologists--Iraq--Basrah--Biography. I Ryding, Karin C.

PJ6064.K5E27 1998
492.7'092--dc21
[1]
ISBN 0-87840-663-8 (cloth) 97-37420

Contents

Foreword

"Classical Arabic literature is the enduring monument of a civilization, not of a people." Thus the distinguished Arabist/Islamicist, the late Sir Hamilton Gibb, opened the first chapter of his masterly *Arabic Literature*. Cultural analysts after him are likely to say the same about Arabic philosophy, historiography, and other constituents of medieval Islamic civilization.

The element of truth in Gibb's statement is evident, but it is one of those generalizations that is liable to be misunderstood in that it could suggest to the unwary student of Islamic civilization that the Arabs were not one of the architects of that civilization but that other ethnic groups were, such as the Persians, who indeed contributed a series of giants on whose shoulders medieval Islam partly rests in many of its constituents.

The Arabs, however, were the ethnic group that spread Islam, whose Prophet, Muḥammad, was an Arab and whose Holy Book, the Qur'ān, was revealed in Arabic, the language of medieval Islamic civilization. It is, therefore, of some importance to identify the share of the Arabs in the rise of this civilization, especially as they were strongly aware of their identity as Arabs, and this awareness went back to the pre-Islamic period. The Arabs kept their ethnocentricity in Islamic times and the fact is even evidenced by the rise of the *shu'ūbiyya* movement, a reaction that sought to glorify the non-Arabs in medieval Islamic society at the expense of the Arabs. Arab awareness of ethnic identity has been enhanced in modern time with the rise of nationalism throughout the Muslim world and the old term *'urūba* has been endowed with a more sophisticated modern content. Thus students of Islamic civilization can, with some justification, reexamine it along these lines in order to find out the contribution of each of the ethnic groups that made up medieval Islamic society.[1]

Within this framework, this reexamination will reveal that the Arab contribution was considerable, and it will suffice to examine two facets of medieval Islamic civilization: philosophy and history. The principal philosophers of Islam are four: al-Kindī, al-Fārābī, Ibn Sīnā, and Ibn Rushd. Two of these four were Arabs, al-Kindī and Ibn Rushd. Moreover, it was al-Kindī who laid the foundation of subsequent philosophical thought in medieval Islamic times. In historiography, al-Mas'ūdī, in the opinion of one who should know, Ibn Khaldūn, was *imām al-mu'arrikhīn, "the imām* of the historians," and his works are true historiography, much more than those of the encyclopedic al-Ṭabarī or al-Baladhūrī, and he was an Arab. And so was Ibn Khaldūn himself, the philosopher of history and one of the glories of medieval Islam, whose significance transcends the frontiers of the Islamic world. The brilliant civilization of Spanish Islam, which lasted for eight centuries, was with few exceptions almost entirely Arab with its array of poets, historians, philosophers, and scientists.

The figure whom this book celebrates belongs to this ethnic group. He was an Arab of the Arabs who hailed from Oman and who belonged to that tribal group -- the Azd, which played an important role in the history of the Arabs before and after the rise of Islam. Al-Khalīl's achievements clinch the claim of the Arabs to be the founders of the science of philology in medieval Islam. Although the Introduction to this volume and the various contributions in it indicate al-Khalīl's place in this discipline, a few observations on him may be made in the restricted context of this Foreword, which relate to cultural analysis rather than to linguistics:

1. Al-Khalīl's versatility and the diversity of his achievements have often been commented upon, but he remains basically a philologist, and what is striking about his achievement in this area is its *comprehensiveness*; witness his contributions to phonology, grammar, and lexicography. Furthermore, he took on not only Arabic prose but also Arabic verse to which he also contributed a "grammar," namely, its metrics or prosody. Those who have studied his works have noted that he also investigated music, but that his work in this field was not outstanding; however, it is possible that his interest was not in music *per se* but was derivative from his interest in language -- language rhythmically expressed in verse. If so, then this calls for a reevaluation of his work on music as really preparatory for his work on metrics. It reflects well on al-Khalīl that his approach to the study of the rhythm of language in verse was a *disciplined* one, that is, he came to it from the world of rhythm, namely, music, which he investigated for the better understanding of the musicality of Arabic verse -- a verse system that lends itself to such treatment since it is exceptionally rhythmical. That the *'arūḍ-īqā'* theory is under fire[2] does not diminish the value of al-Khalīl's approach, which, as has been said, was distinguished by its disciplined character.

Thus, the Arabic language in its entirety (both prose and verse) became the object of al-Khalīl's extensive research. The durability of his achievement is truly astounding since Arabic grammar, lexicography, and prosody are now essentially where he left them twelve hundred years ago.

2. Originality: al-Khalīl was what the Arabs called *mubtadi'*, "creative, inventive," not *muttabi'*, "follower, imitator." Grammar is usually associated with the name of Sībawayh, whose book, *al-Kitāb*, became, and rightly so, the standard work on Arabic grammar. But

in this Sībawayh was a *muttabi'* and not a *mubtadi'* ; he was the student of al-Khalīl and a large portion of the grammatical statements in *al-Kitāb* are those of his master, al-Khalīl, by his own admission. If al-Khalīl's primacy in grammar is contested by admirers of Sībawayh, there can be no contention about his place in the history of Arabic lexicography and prosody of which he was truly the founder. The cultural analysis of the Arab/Muslim humanities, therefore, has in al-Khalīl a genius of the first order both in his originality and the vastness of his *oeuvre*, and so he may be added to what the Arabs call *al-awā'il*, that is, "the firsts" in their respective contributions.

3. Al-Khalīl was not only an Arab, but was also a Muslim, and a pious, ascetic one at that. As a Muslim he was aware of the fact that the *'arabiyya* he was investigating was the language of the Qur'ānic Revelation; that God had chosen the Arabic language for His last Revelation and that the Qur'ānic *i'jāz*, a dogma of paramount importance, was inextricably linked to its language. It is difficult not to believe -- and it is touching -- that al-Khalīl must have thought that in pursuing his philological investigation, he was also performing a task that was an act of piety, *ad maiorem Dei gloriam*. Nothing illustrates the truth of this statement better than the manner of his death. It was in a mosque that he died when he collided with one of its pillars, while preoccupied with scanning some Arabic verses or clarifying some arithmetical concepts. The *ḥadīth*, "the ink of the scholar is better than the blood of the martyr," *ḥibru al-'ālim khayrun min dami al-shahīd*, may thus be applied to him with especial appropriateness, since not only one of the two terms of the *ḥadīth* but both are applicable to him, the scholar and martyr that he was, and, what is more, martyr of his *'ilm*. Thus the strong religious sentiment he was possessed of may be conceived as the animating and unifying force behind his endeavors on behalf of Arabic. And yet despite this, his approach and treatment of Arabic remained as rigorously scientific

as any of the secular linguists/philologists of modern times.

4. Al-Khalīl's achievements are especially significant in a civilization such as medieval Islam was, a *kitāb*-centered civilization, both in the sense of being Qur'āno-centric and in the sense that literature became its distinguishing feature, overshadowing its other facets. But language is the medium of literature; hence the achievements of al-Khalīl pertained not to the periphery but to the center of the edifice of Islamic civilization. Arabic was then, and still is, the language of the Holy Book, the Qur'ān, and of worship throughout the Muslim world, both Arab and non-Arab; in medieval times it was also the language of Islamic civilization from India to Spain; and in modern times it is of the Arab world from the Arabian Gulf to the Atlantic Ocean. It was this vastly spread language and linguistic medium that al-Khalīl's wide-ranging intellectual curiosity investigated. So, just as he himself is central in the history of the Arabic language, so is the language he successfully investigated central in both the structure of Arabic medieval civilization and of the Arabs in modern times.

Finally, it may be remembered that al-Khalīl hailed from Oman -- that Arab/Muslim country that has always been strongly aware of its identity and of its rich cultural heritage throughout the ages. Al-Khalīl was one of her sons, and the Sultanate can, therefore, take legitimate and justifiable pride in this son of hers, al-Khalīl ibn Aḥmad al-Farāhīdī al-Azdī, "the man created of gold and musk," her enduring gift to the Arab and the Muslim world.[3]

Irfan Shahîd

Notes

1. This paragraph has not been written as a sop to the National Cerberus; it is an engagement in a purely academic dialogue with the *shu'ūbiyya.*

2. See the contribution of Eckhard Neubauer in this volume.

3. That Ibn Durayd, the author of *Jamharat al-lugha,* was another Omani, who, though born in Basra, traced his lineage to the Azd of Oman, redounds to the greater glory of the Sultanate. On Ibn Durayd and the *Jamharat*, see the contribution of Ramzi Baalbaki, also in this volume.

Preface and Acknowledgments

This set of essays was conceived to commemorate the name and achievements of al-Khalīl ibn Aḥmad al-Farāhīdī, who resided in Basra in the eighth century, A.D., and who was an individual of wide-ranging talent, interests, and intellect. Al-Khalīl was distinguished in his own time as a lexicographer, phonologist, grammarian, and educator. In the Arab world, he is remembered principally for two achievements: the creation of the first dictionary of the Arabic language (*Kitāb al-'ayn*, "The Book of *'Ayn*") and discovery of the rule-governed metrical systems used in pre-Islamic Arabic poetry. However, his biographers also cite publications on musical theory and have preserved fragments of his poetry. In addition to these achievements, he was also the teacher of the medieval Islamic world's distinguished authority on Arabic grammar, 'Umar ibn 'Uthmān ibn Qanbar Sībawayh (d. ca. A.H. 180/A.D. 796).

Al-Khalīl is an appropriate figure on which to focus scholarly interest for a number of reasons. He represents the formative and perhaps most intellectually challenging period of Arabic language science, A.D. 750-800, and, as Carter has put it in his essay in this volume, is "one of the most original and stimulating personalities to have emerged within the authentically Arab-Islamic tradition of scholarship." Al-Khalīl's death date is usually cited as between A.H. 170-177/ A.D. 786-793. This volume is in tribute to his memory as a founder of 1,200 years of the Arabic linguistic and scholarly tradition.

The contents of this book represent contributors from the Middle East, Europe, and America, each of whom has approached al-Khalīl from a different perspective, focusing on al-Khalīl the linguist, the poet, or the musicologist. These articles provide a broad perspective on his talents, character, and fields of interest, which is what was originally aimed for, inasmuch as al-Khalīl's achievements are little known outside the Arab world. There has been one biography in Arabic, and published editions in Arabic, of what remains of written grammatical and lexicographical work attributed to him (*Kitāb al-ʿayn, al-Jumal fī al-naḥw, Maʿāni al-Ḥurūf*).[1] However, since he was interested in other domains besides these, it seemed that to grasp the scope of al-Khalīl's work, an interdisciplinary approach was warranted.

A standard Arabic transliteration system is used for words and text taken from Arabic sources, including names of individuals. For place names and other terms in Arabic that have conventional spellings in English, those spellings are normally used (e.g., Oman rather than ʿUmān, Abbasid rather than ʿAbbāsid). An exception is the term Qurʾān, which is used instead of the conventional English spelling, Koran.

Originally planned in 1989, this volume represents the work of several distinguished scholars, but the first individual to thank is Professor Irfan Shahîd, Islamic Sultanate of Oman Professor of Arabic and Islamic Literature at Georgetown University, and mentor of this project. It is thanks to his interest, enthusiasm, and unwavering support that this book came into being. I am profoundly indebted to him for his assistance in contacting contributors and in advising me throughout the process of editing and publication.

I would also like to express appreciation to Dr. Barbara

Stowasser, Director of the Center for Contemporary Arab Studies, and Dr. James E. Alatis, Dean Emeritus of the School of Languages and Linguistics, who encouraged and supported me in every way. Professor Kees Versteegh, of the University of Nijmegen, kindly read, corrected, and commented on early drafts of the Introduction, and I am grateful for his astute observations and assistance. Dr. Zainab Taha was a valuable and indefatigable resource for my own contribution, researching knotty points of the Arabic poetic citations, and reviewing my translation. Dr. Aida Bamiya of the University of Florida, and Editor of *al-'Arabiyya*, was very supportive and helpful in reviewing the manuscript. Two anonymous referees also contributed valuable comments and corrections. Dr. Richard Schwartz, Dean of the Graduate School at Georgetown, John Samples, Director of Georgetown University Press, and the staff of the Press also have my sincere thanks for their interest, advice, and support of this project.

My administrative assistant, Jennifer Brandeen, helped me immeasurably in formatting and word-processing the text. Others to thank include Kathleen Borowski, Richard Dorn, Karen Lautman, Michelle Miller, and Paul Roochnik. Without their alert, sophisticated, and diligent workmanship, I would not have been able to produce the manuscript.

To the contributors I extend special thanks, not only for the outstanding quality of their research and analysis, but also because they were extremely patient, understanding, and kind when my house burned down in 1991 and I lost my library, notes, and work. Recovery from this calamity occupied me for the better part of four years, during which this project had to be postponed. I am pleased that it has now come to fruition.

Note

1. For the biography, see Mahdi Makhzūmi, *al-Khalīl ibn Aḥmad al-Farāhīdī: a'māluhu wa-manhajuhu* (Baghdad, 1960). Edited versions of al-Khalil's work include: Ramaḍān 'Abd al-Tawwāb, ed., *Ma'ānī al-Ḥurūf* (Cairo, 1969); Mahdī Makhzūmi and Ibrāhīm al-Samarrā'i, eds., *Kitāb al-'ayn*, 7 vols. (Baghdad, 1980-85); and Fakhr al-Dīn Qabāwa, ed., *Kitāb al-jumal fī al-naḥw* (Beirut, 1985). As this book goes to press, I have just received Professor Qabāwa's revised and expanded edition of *al-Jumal.*

Introduction

Although al-Khalīl ibn Aḥmad is a widely respected Arabic language authority of almost legendary proportions, Western scholars in particular have been hampered in their appreciation of his work by the sparseness and dispersion of information on his achievements. Moreover, although a number of works were ascribed to him by Arab biographers and encyclopedists, few have survived. Some of those works that have surfaced and have been published in scholarly editions in recent years are still not definitively established as his products.[1] This volume aims at assembling and analyzing core data relating to al-Khalīl while providing a stimulus and resource for further research into his works and his theories. Although researchers may not agree on interpretation of the data, the initiation of a critical dialogue based on stringent investigation of sources is a step toward understanding this central figure in Arabic language history and in filling the need for interpretation of original sources.

A Brief Biography

"Whoever should wish to look at a man created of gold and musk, let him look at al-Khalīl ibn Aḥmad."[2]

Al-Sirāfī gives his full name as al-Khalīl ibn Aḥmad Abū ʻAbd al-Raḥmān al-Farāhīdī al-Azdī; Abū Ṭayyib al-Lughawī gives it as al-Khalīl ibn Aḥmad al-Furhūdī and discusses the origin of the name at some length.[3] Qifṭī gives the full name as al-Khalīl ibn Aḥmad ibn

'Abd al-Raḥmān Abū 'Abd al-Raḥmān al-Farāhīdī al-Azdī, and Suyūṭī gives it as al-Khalīl ibn Aḥmad ibn 'Amr ibn Tamīm al-Farāhīdī al-Baṣrī, Abū 'Abd al-Raḥmān.[4]

By all accounts al-Khalīl was a gifted individual, but also introverted, pious, and ascetic, with minimal material needs or ambitions, who concentrated almost exclusively on the life of the mind.[5] His family origins were in Oman, but he was raised in Basra and spent most of his life there, studying philology under the two most distinguished Arabic scholars of that period: 'Īsā ibn 'Umar al-Thaqafī (d. A.H. 149/A.D. 766) and Abū 'Amr ibn al-'Alā' (d. A.H. 155/A.D. 771).[6] Qifṭī reports that al-Naḍr ibn Shumayl (d. A.H. 203/A.D. 818), one of al-Khalīl's students said: "He lived in a house made of Basran reeds, without a penny, his colleagues earning money with [what they learned of] his knowledge; I heard him say: "When I shut my door, my concern does not go beyond it."[7]

As Carter notes in his essay, al-Khalīl refused lucrative official positions and patronage in order to devote himself to scholarship. According to one anecdote, when approached by the emissary of Sulaymān ibn 'Alī of Aḥwaz with the proposition that he become the tutor of his child, al-Khalīl brought out a crust of dry bread which he offered to the emissary saying: "Eat, for I have nothing else, and as long as I have it [dry bread], there is [on my part] no need for Sulaymān." The emissary reportedly asked: "What shall I report to Sulaymān [from you]?" and al-Khalīl responded with an extemporaneous quatrain, the third line of which is: "Poverty is in the soul; not in property shall you encounter it; likewise are riches in the soul and not in property."[8]

The traditional account of his demise also illustrates the extent to which al-Khalīl absorbed himself in mental activity. Qifṭī reports that al-Khalīl wanted to clarify some arithmetical concepts for his servant girl so that the grocer would not be able to cheat her. He entered the mosque, preoccupied with that particular problem, and he inadvertently collided with a pillar. "He fell on his back, and that was the reason for his death." Some say, continues Qifṭī, that al-Khalīl was scanning verses (rather than thinking about grocery bills) "but only God knows which of the two things it was."[9]

Al-Khalīl's wide-ranging intellect, power of concentration, and intuition revealed themselves in his discoveries and expositions on music, prosody, phonology, grammar, and lexicology. He was the first to ascertain and analyze the metric system of pre-Islamic poetry, labeling many of the meters with names they bear to this day; he designed the first Arabic dictionary (*Kitāb al-ʿayn*),[10] discovered and described the phonotactic rules of Arabic lexical root morphemes, and taught Arabic grammar to a number of pupils, including the individual whose work emerged as the apotheosis of that field, Sībawayh.[11]

Al-Khalīl was, therefore, a profound, indefatigable, and incisive thinker, teacher, and author, known even during his lifetime for his erudition, integrity, self-discipline, and insight. Ibn al-Anbārī reports that he was: "master of the literati, one and all, in his knowledge and his asceticism, and the greatest in the establishment of correct analogy [*taṣḥīḥ al-qiyās*]."[12] Sellheim in *The Encyclopaedia of Islam* states that "By his comprehensive studies and intensive teachings al-Khalīl promoted decisively the already existing beginnings of Arabic philology, and thus became its real founder."[13]

Many Arabic biographers confirm, along the lines of Ibn al-Anbārī, that "most of the narrative in the *Kitāb* of Sībawayh is from al-Khalīl; and every time Sībawayh says: 'I asked him,' or: 'he said,' without identifying the speaker, he [is referring to] al-Khalīl ibn Aḥmad."[14]

The Basran Cultural Milieu

Mesopotamia was the cradle of ancient civilizations, including the Sumerian, Babylonian, and Assyrian. Prior to the Arab conquest in the seventh century, it had constituted a part of the Parthian, Roman, Byzantine, and Persian (Sassanid) empires, and in the seventh and eighth centuries, it was fertile ground for the growth not only of the Islamic empire as a political entity but also of Arabic intellectual life, culture, and commerce. The towns of Kufa, Basra, Baghdad, and nearby Jundishapur formed a regional nucleus into which filtered the ideas, expertise, skills and traditions of the many lands and civilizations for which Mesopotamia was a land bridge.

The garrison town of Basra, founded in A.H. 17/A.D. 638 by Caliph ʻUmar ibn al-Khaṭṭāb (d. A.H. 23/A.D. 644), located near the confluence of the Tigris and Euphrates where they form the Shaṭṭ al-ʻArab and flow into the Arabian Gulf, was a cosmopolitan crossroads for Byzantine, Indian, Persian, and Arab cultures. Originally settled by Arab soldiers who came in several waves, many bringing their families, Basra subsequently became a target of gradual migration for people from the Hijaz, from Oman, and from Najd, so that only fifty years after its founding, its population had reached 300,000. Among the tribes that sent settlers to Basra were the Quraysh, Kināna, Thaqīf, Bāhila, Bakr ibn Wāʾil, ʻAbd al-Qays and Azd.[15]

In addition to the great waves of Arab settlers, according to Makhzūmi, there were a number of other ethnic groups who settled in colonies in and around the Basra area, including Indians, Javanese, Sudanese, Zanzibaris, and Greeks, as well as the indigenous Aramaean and Persian elements. Agriculture and fishing were substantial industries, but international commerce was the most important source of income. "Commerce was not limited to material profits, for the Basrans acquired expertise and sophistication; their minds were immersed in the tincture of science, their language was stamped with a special imprint."[16] It was in Basra that initial efforts were made to extract and articulate rules of Arabic language structure, beginning, as tradition has it, with Abū al-Aswad al-Duʾalī (d. A.H. 69/A.D. 688).[17] It became the seat of Arabic language research for the next two centuries, although it had to share its fame with that of Kufa, where another school of grammar evolved, often termed a "rival" entity, but which seems to have differed from the orthodox school in Basra more in philosophy and approach than in actual linguistic practice.[18]

Early Islamic Science

From what is known of this eighth century period, it is one of extraordinary intellectual activity. George Sarton, in his classic, multivolume *Introduction to the History of Science*, labels the era A.D. 750-800, "The Time of Jābir ibn Ḥayyān," (Sarton 1927, 1:520) naming it after the famous but controversial Arab alchemist whose works, dates, and even identity are still debated, not because of the paucity of material attributed to him (quite the contrary), but because of the difficulty of authentication and attribution of that material.[19] Moreover, "with the sole exception of [Alcuin]," states Sarton, "all of the mathematical and astronomical work of this period was done by Muslims."[20]

Intercultural Influences: Syncretism

Sarton's observations lead to what has been a controversial issue in the reconstruction of the scholarship of this period: the role, form, and timing of foreign (especially Greek) elements in the development of medieval Arabic thought. Although Sarton viewed the transmission and assimilation of Greek, Persian, and Indian cultural influences as ongoing and interactive throughout this period, a traditional Orientalist approach has been to assume that there was a strictly sequenced periodization of stages of the transmission process which began only around the turn of the ninth century A.D. with the establishment, under the Abbasid Caliph, al-Maʾmūn (A.H. 197/A.D. 813 - A.H. 218/A.D. 833), of a full-fledged, officially endorsed movement to translate the classic works of the Greek scientific tradition into Arabic.[21] This linear, sequential periodization theory has now been called into question not only by Sarton (1927), but much more recently by Saliba, Morelon, and --- as regards language science in particular -- Versteegh.[22]

During the pre-Islamic period, i.e., the Roman and Byzantine eras, there was already a "considerable degree of acculturation and assimilation to Graeco-Roman civilization."[23] Contrary to what is generally believed in the West, Arab civilization was involved in the development of an advanced form of urban culture in cities such as Hira, contrasting in lifestyle with the more widely known (and perhaps romanticized) nomadic elements. This Romanized, Hellenized urban component of Arab civilization is often overlooked, but is an essential constituent of the classical cultural heritage, particularly in view of its bi- (or multi-) lingualism and its importance as a bridge between Arab and Greek cultures.[24] It is, therefore, not inconceivable that even eighth century Arabic scholars were exposed to and aware of other scholastic traditions, especially the Greek.[25]

Disciplinary Distinctions

During the early stages of Islamic science, a distinction arose between what were considered "Arab" sciences: theology, jurisprudence, Qurʾānic exegesis, Qurʾānic criticism, *ḥadīth* (the sayings of the Prophet), literature, rhetoric, lexicology, and grammar -- and what were considered "foreign" sciences: alchemy, astronomy, geometry, music, philosophy, and medicine.[26] Whereas the foreign sciences were solidly established in Byzantine and Persian cultures, the Arab sciences were just beginning to delineate themselves, and were in various stages of preparadigmatic data collection, discussion, controversy, and intellectual tension. During this early period of growth, as T.S. Kuhn points out, sciences will ordinarily be more reflective of their general social and cultural context than they are later, when their practitioners are carrying on an established and most likely esoteric tradition.[27] It appears that there was, therefore, despite the dichotomy between Arab and foreign disciplines, wide-ranging interdisciplinary curiosity and a vast absorptive capacity on the part of scholars in many fields, especially the ones which were just beginning to delineate their disciplinary scope and procedures.[28]

This era was consequently a fertile time for the development and articulation of scientific systems, and it has been viewed as a period where the protosciences of antiquity were transformed into more sophisticated and data-based disciplines. As Aldo Mieli writes in *La science arabe*: "Le milieu du VIIIe siècle de notre ère peut être considéré comme un tournant très remarquable dans l'histoire du monde et... on peut le prendre pour limite entre deux périodes bien différentes qui s'opposent, tout en se continuant."[29]

Al-Khalīl's Role

Al-Khalīl undoubtedly played a formative role in the development and definition of Arabic language science. He was a pivotal personality, an authority who interacted with and influenced the scope, standards, and quality of the scholarship of his time. His intellect seems to have been one which absorbed and digested sophisticated disciplinary traditions from many other cultures as well as Arabic.[30]

Judging from the range of al-Khalīl's talents and interests, he must have had particularly acute perception of sounds and their interrelationships. His insights into the phonotactic rules of Arabic morphological roots, grasp of phonological structure, analysis of poetic meter, and interest in music together reflect an ability to extract and identify sound patterns and relationships within various conceptual systems. An intermapping, interdisciplinary skill emerges as a central feature in his scholarly endeavors. This kind of context-independent cognitive process may also be one reason for al-Khalīl's apparent superiority in reasoning by analogy, inasmuch as analogy is "a way of focusing on relational commonalities independently of the objects in which those commonalities are embedded."[31]

Given that the surviving testimony to his scholarship is limited and fragmented, it is hoped that the contributions in this book will serve to further awareness of his intellectual activities and to expand understanding of his legacy.

The Contributions

Since these essays touch on al-Khalīl's life and works in diverse ways, it is not possible to pull them together thematically here in the Introduction as would be expected with essays on a limited theoretical topic. Each of the contributions to this volume is a case study of some aspect of al-Khalīl's scholarship, his influence, or his character.

There are four articles, in addition to the Introduction. The identified objective was to deal with al-Khalīl from a number of angles in order to bring his work into perspective for a Western audience that would include Arabists and non-Arabists alike. The contributors, through their mobilization of a range of topics and sources, have provided a rich array of information and breadth of critical evaluation. These essays are constellated around al-Khalīl, but they offer as well a historical contextualization for his work that embraces a spectrum of medieval Arabic intellectual activity: music, poetry, grammar, and lexicography.

The essay by Michael G. Carter is a prosopography that constructs, perhaps for the first time, a coherent picture of al-Khalīl through analysis and subsequent synthesis of a wide range of sources. He takes a cultural and literary perspective focusing on how al-Khalīl developed into "an ideal prototype of the learned Muslim," thereby providing insight not only into the character of his subject, but also into the scholarly and ethical values of the early Abbasid era.

Ramzi Baalbaki has chosen to investigate a long-standing debate in Arabic lexicography -- whether the *Jamharat al-lugha* dictionary by Ibn Durayd (d. A.H. 321/A.D. 933) is a plagiarized version of al-Khalīl's *Kitāb al-ʿayn*, or whether it is a distinctive, original work. He offers a meticulously researched and documented comparative study of the two works that analyzes the aims, approach, and contents of each composition. He contrasts them in all these respects, bringing order out of an area where previously there existed only fragmentary and impressionistic data.

Eckhard Neubauer tackles one of the most challenging aspects of al-Khalīl studies, his contributions to Arabic music and music theory. Although books on music theory are attributed to him by some biographers, none of these works has survived, and Neubauer extrapolates elements of al-Khalīl's music theory through scrupulous examination of contemporary source materials, especially those pertaining to his predecessor, Yūnus al-Kātib (d. ca. A.H. 147/A.D. 765) and his successor, Isḥāq ibn al-Mawṣilī (d. A.H. 235/A.D. 850).

This reconstruction and evaluation of al-Khalīl's activities in music is an important contribution both to the study of early medieval music theory and to the legacy of al-Khalīl.[32]

My own contribution takes the form of a translation and commentary on one of the sections of *al-Jumal fī al-naḥw*, a grammatical text on desinential inflection attributed to al-Khalīl. The attribution to al-Khalīl is not without problems in terms of the text's title, its metalanguage, and its content. Therefore, examination of the text is aimed at stimulating further commentary, clarification, and evaluation. If even some elements of this text can be traced to al-Khalīl, then it adds to our knowledge of his work.

Karin C. Ryding

Notes

1. Controversy has centered on two issues in particular: first, whether al-Khalīl can be considered the compiler of all the entries in the *Kitāb al-ʿayn*, and second, whether or not he was the author of the *Kitāb al-jumal fī al-naḥw*. As regards the first, see John Haywood, *Arabic Lexicography* (Leiden, 1965) and Stefan Wild, *Das Kitāb al-Ain und die arabische Lexikographie* (Wiesbaden, 1965). Note also Rudolph Sellheim, "al-Khalīl ibn Aḥmad," in the *Encyclopaedia of Islam* (2d. ed.) vol. 4 (Leiden, 1978).

As regards the second issue, see Fakhr al-Dīn Qabāwa's introduction to his edition of al-Khalīl's *Kitāb al-jumal fī al-naḥw* (Beirut, 1985) and his considerably expanded introduction to the fifth edition (Beirut [?], 1995). Although this latest edition was received too late to incorporate its findings into the present volume, Qabāwa has added two more manuscript versions to his comparative study and now leans even more firmly toward al-Khalīl as the author. Compare Qabāwa's research and conclusions with that of Fuat Sezgin, *Geschichte des arabischen Schrifttums*, vol. 9, *Grammatik*, 47; and Jonathan Owens, *Early Arabic Grammatical Theory: Heterogeneity and Standardization*, (Philadelphia, 1990), 7, 189-190. See also Karin C. Ryding, "Morphosyntactic Analysis in *al-jumal fii l-naHw*: Discourse Structure and Metalanguage," in Ellen Broselow, Mushira Eid, and John McCarthy, eds., *Perspectives on Arabic Linguistics IV* (Philadelphia, 1992), 263-277; Karin C. Ryding, review of *Early Arabic Grammatical Theory*, by Johnathan Owens, *Historiographia Linguistica* 19 (1992), 393-399.

2. *man aḥabba an yanẓura ilā rajulin khuliqa mina l-dhahab wa-l-misk fa-l-yanẓur ilā l-Khalīl ibn Aḥmad.* Attributed to the ascetic traditionalist Ṣufyān al-Thawrī of Kufa (d. A.H. 162/A.D. 778), as quoted by Makhzūmi, *al-Khalil*, 42; and also by Abū Bakr Kamāl al-Dīn 'Abd al-Raḥmān ibn Muḥammad Ibn al-Anbārī, *Nuzhat al-alibbā' fī tabaqāt al-udabā'*, ed. Muḥammad Abū Faḍl Ibrāhīm (Cairo, n.d.), 47.

3. Abū Sa'īd al-Ḥasan ibn 'Abd Allāh al-Sirāfī, *Akhbār al-naḥwiyyīn al-baṣriyyīn*, ed. Muḥammad Ibrāhīm al-Bunna (Cairo, 1985), 54; 'Abd al-Waḥīd ibn 'Alī Abū al-Ṭayyib al-Lughawī al-Ḥalabī, *Marātib al-naḥwiyyīn*, ed. M. Abū Faḍl Ibrāhīm (Cairo, 1955, 1974), 54-55.

4. 'Alī ibn Yūsuf al-Qifṭī, *Inbāh al-ruwāh 'alā anbāh al-nuḥāt*, ed. M. Abū Faḍl Ibrāhīm, vol. 1 (Cairo, 1950), 341; al-Ḥāfiẓ Jamāl al-Dīn 'Abd al-Raḥmān al-Suyūtī, *Bughyat al-wu'āt fī tabaqāt al-lughawiyyīn wa-al-nuḥāt*, ed. M. Abū Faḍl Ibrāhīm, v 1 (Cairo, 1964), vol. 557.

5. *wa kāna l-khalīl 'afīf al-nafs; lā yakhtāru ṣuḥbat al-mulūk wa-l-umarā'.* "Al-Khalīl was virtuous of spirit, not choosing (either) the companionship of kings or princes" (Qifṭī, *Inbāh*, 344). Also: *kāna mina l-zuhhād fī l-dunyā wa-l-munqaṭi'īna ilā l-'ilm,* "He was one of the world's ascetics, dedicated exclusively to knowledge." (Sirāfī, *Akhbār*, 55).

6. For an outline of his study with al-Thaqafī, see Ṣabāḥ 'Abbās al-Salīm, *'Īsā ibn 'Umar al-Thaqafī: naḥwuhu min khilāl qirā'atihi* (Baghdad/Beirut, 1975), 61-63.

7. Qifṭī, *Inbāh*, 345.

8. *wa-l-faqru fī l-nafsi lā fī al-māli ta'rifuhu*
wa-mithlu dhaka l-ghinā fī l-nafsi lā l-māli

(Ibn al-Anbārī, *Nuzhat al-alibbā'*, 47). See also a close version of this story in Sirāfī, *Akhbār*, 55 and Zubaydī, *Tabaqāt*, 47.

9. Qifṭī, *Inbāh*, 346.

10. For the most part, it is thought that al-Khalīl composed the introduction to the dictionary, compiled the first chapter, and originated the system of arrangement of entries (perhaps influenced by the Indian alphabetical system), which is based on the point of articulation of phonemes, the farthest back (the pharyngeal) being the Arabic *'ayn*. Thus all lexical roots containing an *'ayn* (in whatever position) would be listed first, then those with *ḥā'*, and so on. The complete compilation of this first of all Arabic dictionaries, however, is thought to have been accomplished by al-Khalīl's disciple al-Layth ibn al-Muẓaffar. See Abū al-Faraj Muḥammad ibn Isḥāq ibn Muḥammad ibn Isḥāq ibn al-Nadīm, *Fihrist*, ed. and trans. Bayard Dodge, (New York, 1970), 94-96; Fuat Sezgin, *Geschichte des arabischen Schrifttums*, vol. 8, *Lexikografie* (Leiden, 1982), 51-56; Wild, *Das Kitāb al-Ain*, 14-16; and Haywood, *Arabic Lexicography*, 11-40, for further discussion of this point.

11. Abū Bishr 'Amr ibn 'Uthmān ibn Qanbar Sībawayh, *Kitāb Sībawayh fī al-naḥw* (*Le livre de Sibawaihi*), ed. Hartwig Derenbourg, 2 vols., reprint of 1881 edition (Hildesheim, 1970); also, the more recent version: *Kitāb Sībawayh*, ed. 'Abd al-Salām Muḥammad Hārūn, 5 vols. (Beirut, 1991).

12. The use of the principle of analogy (*qiyās*), especially in the creation and verification of structural patterns, became increasingly important as the fully inflected forms of classical Arabic became less accessible, and as the language adapted itself to new demands in terms of scientific precision, philosophical and administrative concepts, and other features essential to an international imperial mode of communication. For cogent presentation of theories on the origin of the Arabic term, see Michael Carter, "Les origines de la grammaire arabe," *Revue des Études Islamiques*, 40 (1972), 69-97, and C. H. M. Versteegh, "The Origin of the Term 'Qiyas' in Arabic Grammar," *Zeitschrift für Arabische Linguistik* 4 (1980), 7-30.

13. Sellheim, "al-Khalīl ibn Aḥmad," 962.

14. Ibn al-Anbārī, *Nuzhat al-alibbā',* 46.

15. Mahdī Makhzūmi, *al-Khalīl ibn Aḥmad al-Farāhīdī: a'māluhu wa-manhajuhu* (Baghdad, 1960), 7.

16. Makhzūmi, *al-Khalīl ibn Aḥmad,* 8-9.

17. For a thorough overview of the earliest phase of Arabic language analysis, see Rafael Talmon, "Who Was the First Arab Grammarian?" in *Zeitschrift für Arabische Linguistik,* 15 (1985), 128-145.

18. For discussion of differences between the two schools, see Gustav Flügel, *Die grammatischen Schulen der Araber* (Nendeln, Lichtenstein, 1862, 1966); Gotthold Weil, *Die grammatischen Streitfragen der Basrer and Kufer* (which includes Ibn al-Anbārī's Arabic text: *al-Inṣāf* *fī masā'il al-khilāf bayna al-naḥwiyyīn al-baṣriyyīn wa-al-kūfiyyīn)* (Leiden, 1913) and also his *Die grammatischen Schulen von Kufa und Basra* (Leiden, 1913). In English, see Mortimer Sloper Howell's preface to his *Grammar of the Classical Arabic Language*, vol. 1 (New Delhi, 1986) (reprint of 1883 ed.). In Arabic, see Shawqī Ḍayf, *al-Madāris al-naḥwiyya* (Cairo, 1968) and Muḥammad Khayr al- Ḥalawānī, *al-Khilāf al-naḥwi bayn al-baṣriyyīn wa-l-kufiyyīn wa kitāb al-inṣāf* (Aleppo, 1971). To some extent the differences between the two schools seem to have paralleled the analogy/anomaly dispute originally associated with scholars of Alexandria and Pergamum. The Basrans focused on the congruence of language phenomena with the concept of balance that was thought to characterize the natural world, whereas the Kufans were more wide-ranging in their acceptance of irregularities and inconsistencies. See R. H. Robins, "Some Continuities and Discontinuities in the History of Linguistics," in *History of Linguistic Thought and Contemporary Linguistics*, ed. Herman Parret (Berlin, 1976), 16 for a brief description of the Alexandria/Pergamum schools.

19. George Sarton, *Introduction to the History of Science*, vol. 1 (Baltimore, 1927), 520. For more on Jābir, see Paul Kraus, *Jabir ibn Hayyan: Contribution à l'histoire des idées scientifiques dans l'Islam* (Paris, 1942, 1986); Henry Corbin, *L'Alchemie comme art hiératique* (Paris, 1986); Pierre Lory, ed. and trans., *Dix traités d'alchemie* (Paris, 1983). For a tenth-century account, see Ibn al-Nadīm, *Fihrist*, 2:853-855.

20. Sarton, *History of Science*, 1:521. He states elsewhere: "The immense cultural importance of Islam lies in the fact that it brought finally together the two great intellectual streams which had flowed independently in ancient times ... Semitic religion and Greek knowledge." (*The History of Science and the New Humanism* [New Brunswick, N.J., 1988], 83).

21. This movement was centered in the *bayt al-ḥikma,* "house of wisdom," in Baghdad, a library, research, and translation center. For more detail on this topic, see M.G. Balty-Guesdon, "Le *Bayt al-Ḥikma* de Baghdad," *Arabica* 39 (1992), 131-150.

22. Sarton, *History of Science*, vol. 1. George Saliba, in his review of *Oevres d'astronomie*, *Isis* 80 (1989), 688-690, reports that Morelon, in the introduction to this translation of the astronomical works of Thābit ibn Qurra, "raises new questions of extreme cultural significance, and forces a reevaluation of the generally accepted periodization of Arabic astronomy, by presenting evidence that the so-called stages of translation, assimilation, and creativity were in fact taking place at the same time. Indeed, one could even ask whether translation was not undertaken for creative researchers who needed the Greek works to support their own research." As for C. H. M. Versteegh, he points out that the conquest of Hellenized cultures throughout the Middle East, including the centers of Hellenistic education and intellectual activity such as Alexandria, Antioch, and Jundishapur, allowed immediate and direct contact between Arab and Greek cultures which provided for penetration and perpetuation of Greek knowledge through the multilingual, polyglot population of the Levant in particular. He distinguishes "between a direct and an indirect way of transmission, the first one of which was earlier than the second," in terms of Greek influence on Arabic linguistics (*Greek Elements in Arabic Linguistic Thinking* [Leiden, 1977], 1). See also his description of the *voie diffuse* (9). For further discussion, see Max Meyerhof, "On the Transmission of Greek and Indian Science to the Arabs," *Islamic Culture* 9 (1937), 17-29, and Grigoris Ziakas, "On the Problem of the Origin of the Pseudo-Aristotelian Arabic Works," *Graeco-Arabica* 2 (1983), 39-50.

23. Irfan Shahîd, *Rome and the Arabs: A Prolegomenon to the Study of Byzantium and the Arabs* (Washington, 1981), 153.

24. For the history of Arab culture during Roman and Byzantine times, see Shahid, *Rome and the Arabs*, as well as his subsequent publications: *Byzantium and the Arabs in the Fourth Century* (Washington, 1984); *Byzantium and the Arabs in the Fifth Century* (Washington, 1989); and *Byzantium and the Arabs in the Sixth Century*, vol. 1, parts 1 and 2 (Washington, 1995).

25. For a broader but relevant analysis of Greek influence on Arabic sciences, see Ziakas, "Pseudo-Aristotelian Arabic Works."

26. This arrangement partially resembles the later medieval European university distinction between the *trivium* (grammar, logic, and rhetoric) and the *quadrivium* (arithmetic, music, geometry, and astronomy).

27. "As a result, they constitute a special subculture, one whose members are the exclusive audience for, and judges of, each others' work." (Thomas S. Kuhn, *The Essential Tension*, [Chicago, 1977], 119). See also G. L. Bursill-Hall, "Toward a History of Linguistics in the Middle Ages, 1100-1450" in Dell Hymes, ed., *Studies in the History of Linguistics* (Bloomington, Ind., 1974), esp. 85-87, for the interpenetration of idea systems and the importance of the intellectual framework in the development of medieval grammar.

28. "A new concentration of culture was being accomplished with youthful energy in the newly founded cities of Baghdad, Basra, and Kufa -- comparable in many respects to that which had taken place centuries before in Alexandria. Streams of knowledge were converging in the Caliphate from the Byzantine Empire, from Persia, and from India." (Sarton, *History of Science*, 1:523).

29. Aldo Mieli, *La science arabe et son rôle dans l'évolution scientifique mondiale* (Leiden, 1938), 37.

30. For example, Corbin states: "L'amitié d'Ibn al-Moqaffa', le celèbre converti du mazdéisme, pour le grammarien al-Khalīl (ob. 791) avait rendu accessible à celui-ci tout ce qui existait en pehlevi (moyen iranien) concernant la grammaire et la logique." (*Histoire de la philosophie islamique* [Paris,1964], 201). For further discussion of Ibn al-Muqaffa' and al-Khalīl, see Carter's essay in this volume.

31. Dedre Gentner, "The Mechanisms of Analogical Learning," in Stella Vosniadou and Andrew Ortony, eds., *Similarity and Analogical Reasoning* (Cambridge, 1989), 200.

32. In conjunction with Neubauer's article, readers unfamiliar with Arabic metrics may want to consult the chapter on "Metrics" in *The Arabic Linguistic Tradition* by G. Bohas, J.P. Guillaume, and D.E. Kouloughli (London and New York, 1990), which is an excellent summary in English of al-Khalīl's metrical theory.

Another Khalīl, Courtier, Teacher, and Sage

Michael G. Carter

Al-Khalīl is mostly studied for his innovative role in the disciplines of lexicography, metrics, and grammar, but there is another dimension to him which Western scholarship has somewhat neglected, even though it was no less important to medieval Muslims than his strictly scientific achievements. This essay will describe that aspect of al-Khalīl in broad terms and make some suggestions as to how and why it came about that he acquired the literary persona of a courtly and cultured sage: the reader will immediately recognize that the following pages are, in essence, an elaboration of the portrait of al-Khalīl already given by Rosenthal.[1] The exercise is not one of pure biography, and, therefore, questions of historical veracity do not arise: all sources are equally valid testimony of the idealized figure of al-Khalīl which we encounter therein, hence the paper draws more or less indiscriminately upon works extending from the third century A.H. (ninth century A.D.) to the eleventh century A.H. (seventeenth century A.D.).[2] The selection is necessarily incomplete, and like Ibn al-Qifṭī, we must plead that there are plenty of "good stories and interesting anecdotes" about al-Khalīl but simply no space to include them all. What follows is a composite portrait of one of the most original and stimulating personalities to have emerged within the authentically Arab-Islamic tradition of scholarship.

Piety is credited to virtually every scholar by all biographers as a routine courtesy from one good Muslim to another. In the case of al-Khalīl, however, a higher than usual degree of godliness is ascribed, symbolically foreshadowed in the curious fact that his father (*nomen est omen*) was apparently the first person to bear the name Aḥmad since the Prophet![3] Al-Khalīl's sanctity was attested by none less than Sufyān al-Thawrī, his knowledge of the *sunna* was superior to that of all others, in piety he was exceeded only by Ibn ʻAwn, and his practical devotion manifested itself in the performance of pilgrimage and border raids (*ghazw*) every other year.[4] But perhaps the strongest confirmation of al-Khalīl's impeccable character is the acceptance of his single testimony on Arabic usage without the usual apparatus of *isnād* and alternative verification. This remarkable distinction (given Islam's intense preoccupation with accuracy and corroboration in the transmission of information) was granted to only four early Muslim linguists, the others being al-Aṣmaʻī, Abū Zayd al-Anṣārī, Abū ʻUbayda, and Abū Ḥātim al-Sijistānī.[5] That having been said, it is perhaps surprising that for all his knowledge, piety, and integrity there is no evidence that al-Khalīl was himself a notably industrious transmitter of *Ḥadīth*: it appears that only Ibn Māja relates anything from him.[6]

The unworldliness of al-Khalīl is as conspicuous as his religious fervour, attaining a level of asceticism more expected from a holy man than a scientist and teacher. "All the sources agree that he lived an unpretentious and pious life"[7] is an understatement: al-Khalīl lived in a reed hut and subsisted on dry bread, refusing patronage and office,[8] and although he seems to have had contacts with the court, he never pursued the material comfort and professional status that were the common ambition of the learned class in his day. The picture instead is of a man with a whimsical contempt for the world; thus when a friend's sandal thong breaks, he offers his own sandal with the comment that he would be happy to continue barefoot.[9] He broadcasts his indifference to temporal values not only in prose,--"I desire to be among the most exalted of mankind in the eyes of God, the most mediocre in the eyes of mankind and the meanest in my own eyes"[10]--but also in verse.[11] For example:

> Doctors have cured the sick before, and the patient lives, yet the doctor dies.
> Ready yourself for the summons of death, for near at hand it surely lies.[12]

Another composition on the same theme was highly admired by no less than Ibn al-Mu'tazz:

> Night, and the day, months, then more months, year upon year, these are the only measure of our lives.
> Time is our mount, which bears each new thing to decay, into the grave the noble's carcass drives,
> Strips from his plenty the miser's corpse, and bequeathes to other men the jealous husband's wives.[13]

Neither the piety and world-weariness nor the prose and poetry which express them are at all unconventional, however, except for their emanating from a scholar and scientist for whom they might be thought to have hardly any technical relevance. In the remainder of this paper, we shall look more closely at al-Khalīl as an intellectual and teacher with a view to showing--all questions of historical fact aside--how he developed from a very early period into an ideal prototype of the learned Muslim. In the concluding section, it will be argued that this development is an inevitable product of the Islamic concept of the function of science and learning in religion and society.

A notable feature of al-Khalīl's biography is the number of pronouncements he makes concerning the relationship between master and pupil, the duty to impart and acquire knowledge, and the techniques of teaching and learning. Having himself been rescued from the Ibāḍī heresy by a chance remark of his own mentor, "You only discover the error of your teacher when you go to another one,"[14] al-Khalīl was well aware of the master's ethical responsibilities towards his pupil. By the same token, the student himself has a duty to learn, and al-Khalīl has left a number of very interesting observations on this topic, some quasi-proverbial: "He who is content with what he knows is ignorant and he who adds the knowledge of others to his own deserves the epithet of a divine"[15] and some autobiographical: "I have read in books of scholars that a person who shows reticence in seeking knowledge and hangs back is simply donning the garb of ignorance and wearing the veil of stupidity, and whoever continues throughout his days in extreme ignorance will, when summoned to judgment on Resurrection Day, be blind." Also, "I have achieved some of my learning by casting aside modesty between myself and teachers and by throwing off the veil between myself and those whose learning I sought, for whoever pursues knowledge too fastidiously will end up with a meagre share. I find undue delicacy in seeking knowledge to be stupidity which only leads to folly, both of which in turn lead to error."[16]

That the acquisition of knowledge was recognized as a dialectical process is articulated more than once: "The sciences are locks and questions are their keys,"[17] and "Don't be upset by people who hit you with questions. They are just drawing your attention to things you don't know."[18] Among a number of anecdotes on this subject, one is particularly illuminating because it links al-Khalīl's dialectical skills with the guru-like persona of the master which has already been referred to above. One day al-Khalīl is asked a question and spends so long thinking of an answer that the questioner eventually gives up waiting and leaves. Al-Khalīl's companions reproach him for his slowness, and he asks them how they would have replied, meeting their answer with another question and continuing to do so until they also give up and leave! At this point the sources offer two entirely different interpretations. In Ibn al-'Imād's account, al-Khalīl simply declares: "You must think *before* answering: it is wrong to think afterwards. I never give an answer until I know what objections and criticisms it will expose me to."[19] This rather banal response is a pure reflection of the principles and procedures of public debate, *munāẓara*, which have been so illuminatingly discussed by van Ess[20] and offers nothing really stimulating for our purposes.

As reported by Ibn Abī 'Awn, however, al-Khalīl's reply is extremely obscure and therefore potentially much more exciting: "It is bad [!]," he says, "to think too much when answering a question with a statement [which might lead to another question]."[21] This appears to assert exactly the opposite of Ibn al- 'Imād's version, and is either (textually) corrupt nonsense or a far more intriguing display of al-Khalīl's pedagogical style. Although Ibn Abī 'Awn sometimes took editorial liberties with his material,[22] there is no reason to be automatically suspicious of the text here, and al-Khalīl's intentions might be paraphrased as follows: The wise man knows that one question always leads to another, and he seeks to forestall this by providing a final, unanswerable (*muskit*) rejoinder. However, the wise man also knows that there is no final answer to anything and that for ordinary people it is not even worth trying to find it--both the original questioner and all al-Khalīl's friends, for example, showed their unworthiness by their impatient departure. In those circumstances any answer (viz., statement, leading to more questions)[23] will do, and it is a waste of time to think more deeply about it. If this exegesis is correct, al-Khalīl is treating his interlocutors in much the same way as a Sufi shaykh would handle a postulant, and on this occasion they all fail the test.[24]

It happens that a rather similar story is told with none other than Aristotle as the central figure being interrogated in a dream by al-Maʾmūn. After al-Maʾmūn has received each answer with the enquiry, "and then what?", Aristotle abruptly concludes the interview with, "Then there is no 'and then what!'"[25] Leaving aside the probability that this kind of story is a topos,[26] it is certainly worth emphasizing that al-Khalīl has indeed been compared with Aristotle in the Arabic tradition, albeit rather late (A.H. 1080/A.D. 1670) by Ibn al- 'Imād.[27] Without doubt al-Khalīl's behaviour in the previous anecdote has the same motivation as Aristotle's here -- to assert the dominance of the teacher and to demonstrate one of the techniques of control, namely cutting off the discourse when it no longer serves any purpose. With Aristotle this point is reached after a certain number of questions, while al-Khalīl, as a shrewd judge of character, ensures by his long silence that no dialogue at all is possible with the undeserving student and uncomprehending colleagues, who are left to work out for themselves what a trap they have fallen into.

Every good teacher should know how to prevent the obstreperous or stupid pupil from frustrating the pedagogical process, and al-Khalīl provides us with a crude but effective demonstration of his talent which will strike a sympathetic chord in all those who have ever been faced with a dull student who has no hope of improvement but refuses to go away. Al-Khalīl disposed of this nuisance by giving him a verse to scan, knowing that he would be so preoccupied with the (for him) impossible task of scansion that he would not notice the meaning of the verse, viz.,

> If you can't do it, just leave it and move on to something you can do!

Sure enough the poor victim gives up the attempt and departs without ever realizing what has been done to him.[28]

If the equation of al-Khalīl with Aristotle is relatively late, his famous association with Ibn al-Muqaffaʿ is by contrast attested quite early: al-Zubaydī, who died in A.H. 379/A.D. 989, refers to an actual meeting and records their terse reciprocal assessments afterwards: "[Ibn al-Muqaffaʿ] has more knowledge than intelligence," says the one, "[al-Khalīl] has more intelligence than knowledge," says the other.[29] More important, the connection between the two is established as early as the third century A.H. (ninth century A.D.), for example, by several couplings of their names in the works of al-Jāḥiẓ.[30] We are surely justified in treating the rivalry of al-Khalīl and Ibn al-Muqaffaʿ as a reflection of the *shuʿūbiyya* conflict which was at its height in al-Jāḥiẓ time. In that scenario Ibn al-Muqaffaʿ's undoubtedly superior knowledge of Greek and Iranian writings was not enough to save him from the political error of judgment which led to his execution, while al-Khalīl's superior intelligence allowed him to exploit the comparatively slim corpus of indigenous "Islamic" material with creative genius to produce the new sciences of prosody and lexicography, amongst other achievements.

Shuʿūbiyya tendencies do not, in fact, loom very large in the evolution of al-Khalīl's historical personality, but there is one anecdote which can really only be explained in those terms. In it al-Khalīl tells of a conversation among four monarchs about the difficulty of retracting the spoken word: The Persian ruler found he was better able to repudiate what he had not said rather than what he had said; the Roman emperor sometimes regretted the things he said but never the things he had not said; the Chinese sovereign felt that he only remained in control of words until they were uttered and then they controlled him; while the king of India declared himself amazed how a person can say things which are damaging when held against him and useless when not. To cap this extremely interesting tale, al-Khalīl then proceeds to quote verses from native Arabic poetry epitomizing the four principles described. The *shu'ūbiyya* inspiration is umistakable, and it places al-Khalīl squarely in the role of advocate for Arab wordly wisdom equal to that of any other civilization.[31]

The encounter of al-Khalīl with Ibn al-Muqaffa' has a broader resonance which must now be examined. It is not enough to interpret each of them as representatives of indigenous and foreign learning,respectively, though this undoubtedly underlies their symbolic confrontation. Their relationship, however, is more complex than one of mere polarization. It must be remembered that the "foreign" sciences, after their initial rejection, gradually became innocuous, and formerly taboo disciplines, particularly logic and metaphysics, were eventually incorporated into the canon of orthodox Islamic learning. Al-Khalīl, the unimpeachably Muslim, indelibly Arab scholar, is actually shown in the biographies as assuming some of the characteristics of the "foreigner" Ibn al-Muqaffa', preemptively legitimizing, as it were, the coming developments by anchoring them in the period of Islam's primitive institutionalization. In various ways al-Khalīl is seen moving freely in philosophical and theological circles, being received with reverence, and showing familiarity with their ideas. What more significant gesture could be asked for in this regard than the fact that Ḥunayn Ibn Isḥāq is said to have come to al-Khalīl for help in the perfection of his Arabic?[32] And what more effective way can there be of linking al-Khalīl with the new learning than to have him decipher a letter written in Greek, after only a month's scrutiny? The key being (as any good cryptographer would know) that the document was bound to start with some conventional expression, in this case a reference to the name of God![33]

The sources preserve a number of examples of al-Khalīl's excursions into philosophical and theological (*kalām*) discourse. He left an extraordinary discussion of time and contingency in which events are classified as "things which absolutely exist, things which absolutely do not exist, and things which may or may not exist,"[34] an obvious borrowing from pure philosophy and a good specimen of the breadth of al-Khalīl's intellectual appetite. He also makes a tripartite division of time into *ma'hūd* ("familiar," i.e., past), *mashhūd* ("observed," i.e., present), and *maw'ūd* ("promised," i.e., future),[35] which, if it is not merely a literary conceit and display of *saj'*, may represent a native Arab tradition, perhaps offered as a response to a challenge from the *shu'ūbiyya* (or, less likely, as a native equivalent to the three tenses of Greek). On another occasion he has no difficulty demolishing the Qadarī position on the impossibility of two simultaneous principles of action by simply breaking a stick and thus demonstrating that (active) "breaking" and (passive) "being broken" both occur at one time in the same object![36] His friendship with the Mu'tazilī al-Naẓẓām is well attested, and of special interest to us is that the young al-Naẓẓām was brought along by his father to be a pupil of al-Khalīl, but the latter, having subjected the boy to a number of questions, politely concludes that he can teach him nothing, on the contrary, "it would be better if I were to study under him." Such an unlikely humility surely conceals a symbolic dissociation from al-Naẓẓām's eventual heterodoxy.[37]

The joining of the names of al-Khalīl and Ibn al-Muqaffa' also sheds light on another prominent constituent of al-Khalīl's historical character. For all his religious and political aberrance, Ibn al-Muqaffa' remains a highly esteemed figure in literature, as a master of Arabic prose style and especially as an early exponent of the "mirrors for princes" genre in the secretarial tradition which later evolved into a substantial component of the *adab* or literary culture of the Arab-Islamic court. Much of the content of this literature is of a moralizing kind, and al-Khalīl, too, has left numerous examples of his own talent in this field. Some of his observations on friendship, e.g., that you should be grateful to a friend who alerts you to your faults before an enemy does,[38] might almost have come from Ibn al-Muqaffa' himself. The exaggerated politeness of a courtier shows through in al-Khalīl's reply to a man who fears he has not given him enough room: "An inch of ground cannot cramp two close friends, but there is not enough space in the whole wide world for a pair who cannot abide each other."[39] The etiquette of repartee, the ability to respond with both speed and sharpness, are much admired facilities of a courtier, and al-Khalīl displays as much skill as the next man in turning out sententious verses:

> Boors enjoy it best of all when nobles throw their insults smartly back.
> Leaving them unanswered cuts more deeply than returning the attack.[40]

And given al-Khalīl's special involvement with lexicography and phonology, it is perhaps inevitable that he should be the first person to compose a line of verse containing all the letters of the Arabic alphabet![41]

The humour of al-Khalīl was in keeping with the standards of the times, as can be deduced from his answer to the question, "Why is the diminutive of *wāṣil, 'uwayṣil* and not *wuwayṣil*?"- "Because the Arabs did not want to sound like yelping dogs!"[42] When al-Khalīl is rebuked by his friends for sequestering himself for too long, a social *faux pas* again connected with the conventions of the *majlis*, he makes his feelings plain: He had been immersed in the creation of an entire metrical system, so his retort is appropriately couched in the form of a verse full of labyrinthine wordplay:

> If you had the slightest idea what I'm saying, you'd never take issue with my misdemeanor.
> If I didn't know what a game you are playing, I'd certainly take your demeanor amiss, youhaven't the slightest idea what I'm saying, and still you completely mistake my demeanor.
> But knowing the ignorance you are displaying, I won't make of your misdemeanor an issue![43]

To what extent this curious poem conforms with al-Khalīl's own definition of eloquence: *mā qaruba ṭarafāhu wa-ba'uda muntahāhu*, literally, "what has its extremities close together and its end a long way off," will be left to the reader to decide.[44] We may link this incident with another occasion when al-Khalīl was taken to task for remaining silent at the wrong time, where this time he evinces a combination of tactful deference and sharp humor. It is said that al-Khalīl once attended the teaching of Abū 'Amr ibn al-'Alā' with the intention of challenging him to debate, but did not utter a word throughout the session. His companions, obviously surprised, asked al-Khalīl why he remained silent, and his reply was: "He has been a leading scholar for fifty years, and I was afraid he might break down and his reputation in the city be ruined, so I did not speak to him."[45] One must wonder whether this superficially respectful statement is a heroic example of Newtonian modesty, or is al-Khalīl, the expert *adīb*, discreetly claiming superiority?

It is for performances such as these, presumably, that al-Khalīl earns his place in the following tetrad of "four unprecedented and unsurpassed figures, namely Abū Ḥanīfa for his jurisprudence, al-

Khalīl for his *adab*, al-Jāḥiẓ for his authorship and Abū Tammām for his poetry."[46] Al-Tha'ālibī must be taken seriously, and his appraisal can only be interpreted as meaning that al-Khalīl represented the ideal combination of morals, manners, piety, education, literary talent, and scholarly eminence that are all subsumed under the personal qualities of the *adīb*. It is time to consider the possible reasons for this enormous reverence for someone who is largely thought of as a pure technician.

The key to the answer is provided by al-Khalīl himself in his manifest preoccupation with the place of learning and the status of scholars in Islam, of whom he said: "If these people are not saints [*awliyā'*], then God does not have any saints."[47] This forceful assertion that scholars are the best Muslims doubtless reflects without any exaggeration the self-image of this most self-conscious, not to say self-important, community, always aware of the interdependence of knowledge and religion. For al-Khalīl, as we have seen, the implicit ethical responsibility of scholarship was wholeheartedly accepted. "Study what is in your hearts more diligently than memorizing what is in your books,"[48] he advises, elsewhere neatly paralleled by the recommendation, "Make the contents of books your capital and spend what is in your heart."[49] Such pronouncements sum up the fusion of ethical and scientific values which is the ideal of the teaching profession, on whose behalf al-Khalīl is clearly speaking here.

In addition to defining the duty of the individual, whether master or pupil, al-Khalīl further categorizes the whole community according to its "knowledge." Using a scheme of classification which combines Aristotleian dieresis with Arab fondness for wordplay, al-Khalīl divides the population into the man who knows and knows that he knows (a true scholar, to be followed), the man who knows and does not know that he knows (a forgetful person, to be reminded), the man who does not know and knows that he does not know (an ignorant person, to be taught), and the man who does not know and does not know that he does not know (a fool, to be avoided!).[50] As if to reinforce the proposition and confirm its importance for Islamic society, the sources record another, remarkably similar, declaration in which al-Khalīl describes his response to the four categories of man, these being the one who is more learned than himself (from whom he will derive knowledge), the one who is equally learned (with whom he will share his learning), the one who seeks knowledge (whom he will teach, and thereby earn a living!), and the one who thinks he has superior knowledge (to whom he will not even speak).[51]

Using the same fourfold contrast, al-Khalīl revealingly classifies the sciences into (1) those with a theoretical basis (*aṣl*) and a practical application (*far*ʿ), e.g., arithmetic, which is universally accepted as having both, (2) those with a theoretical basis but no application, e.g., astrology, which has no effect whatsoever on the affairs of the world, (3) those with an application but no theoretical foundation, e.g., medicine, for "doctors will go on experimenting until doomsday," and (4) those with neither theoretical basis nor application, namely *jadal*, the rhetoric of disputation and dialectic, a category about which al-Khalīl makes no comment, suggesting that his targets are the *mutakallimūn* and the philosophers.[52] What is significant about this scheme is not its tendentious (and probably anachronistic) anticipation of such writers as al-Fārābī,[53] but the fact that the sciences embraced by this list are all "foreign" (i.e., Greek) sciences and are obviously being subordinated here to principles of Islamic utility. Only a scholar of al-Khalīl's undisputed orthodoxy and intellectual stature could pass a judgment of this comprehensive and authoritative kind.

There is ample evidence that al-Khalīl was well aware of the link between learning and power and the right of the scholar to a place in the court. He was once asked why, if learning is more important than wealth, there were more scholars at the door of the ruler than rulers at the door of the scholar, and he gave an answer which is again reminiscent of the secretarial style of Ibn al-Muqaffaʿ and his ilk: "Because scholars know their duty towards rulers, but rulers do not know their duty towards scholars."[54] In the court, mosque, and *majlis,* al-Khalīl invariably performs impressively in the scholar's principal public pastime, the debate, though not always triumphing, it is fair to record. In one incident he was asked the apparently simple question, Why should anyone learn grammar? to which he replied, "No one should learn more grammar than necessary," meaning, presumably, that grammatical proficiency should match the requirements of the user. But his interlocutor, the Muʿtazilī theologian (*mutakallim*) Abū Shamir,[55] raises the objection that the superfluous thereby becomes necessary since the necessary can only be defined in terms of the superfluous. In one version of the dispute, al-Khalīl is simply reduced to silence by his opponent's remark,[56] but there is more satisfaction for his audience in the account of Ibn ʿAbd Rabbihi, where al-Khalīl has the last word in no uncertain manner with a violent and distinctly improper stream of abuse:

> You wretch! Do you think you can you cut with a sword-blade without striking a blow, or race horses without galloping, or achieve a goal without striving or aiming for it? And even then your efforts can lead to failure and your faint-heartedness to disappointment![57]

In either case it does look as though al-Khalīl really lost this argument, which raises interesting questions about the symbolism: perhaps it shows that mere personal authority was not enough to withstand the systematizing pressures that Islam was by then going through, where logic had begun to make itself useful.

But as this last item suggests, al-Khalīl is not perfect. His human frailty is acknowledged on more than one occasion, the most striking being when he is criticized for not following his own advice to refuse patronage, and he defends himself with the following truculently candid verses:

> Act on my learning, don't learn from my actions; use what I teach and my failings can't hurt you.
> Roll up your sleeves and try harder than I did; judge for yourself between vices and virtue.[58]

This from a man who coined what was to become a proverb: "When a scholar slips up, the drums beat!"[59] The sarcasm of this last observation is matched by the scepticism with which he laconically enumerates the portents of the end of the world: "forgiveness before it is asked, benefit of the doubt before the charge is laid, generosity before the solicitation, issue of the pardon before the reprimand."[60]

As this sketch of al-Khalīl's character is intended to show, the sources depict a many-sided genius of remarkable piety and learning, though not without some cynicism and minor defects. If interpreted as the description of a symbolic figure rather than a strictly historical personage, al-Khalīl can be seen as embodying a number of idealized qualities of the Muslim scholar and teacher. While the details may well be later reconstructions, there is no question that this picture is rooted in truth. Al-Khalīl's creative genius is beyond doubt: even such a prominent rival as al-Kisāʾī acknowledged it,[61] and his scientific innovativeness has never been seriously questioned.[62]

His piety was exemplary, as has already been mentioned: it can be noted additionally that he is one of the four Basrans of the time who did not follow the beliefs of the *ahl al-hawā*,[63] that is to say, in all the ferment of new knowledge to which he was exposed, he was one of the few whose purity of faith was never challenged. His concern for the teaching profession, its values, methods, and goals is extraordinary, and when seen in connection with his outstanding frugality and modesty, his attitude comes close to that of the Sufi master or guru. He was also admired for his virtuosity in prose and poetry and his ready wit, and was no stranger to the world of philosophical and theological debate.

By far the most significant aspect of the literary portrait, however, for which it is now time to suggest an explanation, is the fact that it contains almost nothing of relevance to al-Khalīl's scientific achievements. Apart from the usual anecdotes about the discovery of the metrical system and some remarks on the composition of the *Kitāb al-'ayn*, the biographies have scarcely a word to say on the nature or principles of the sciences, in the foundation of which al-Khalīl played such a creative role.[64] Instead we are shown a man unsurpassed in piety, knowledge of Islam, personal integrity, pedagogical preeminence, courtly manners, and literary brilliance, and the question arises, why is this so? The answer, apart from the obvious one that no such information was preserved, is not to be found in the plausible generalization that all Islamic biographies are of this kind, but is rather to be sought by reversing the question and asking, what exactly is the reason for this characteristic of Islamic biography?

When we consider the essence of the disciplines in which al-Khalīl was so innovative and their crucial importance for Islamic civilization, it becomes obvious that only an individual of unblemished faith and character could be entrusted with such a critical body of knowledge. It is well known that Islam depends, perhaps more than any religion, on the linguistic event of revelation with all its consequences -- the recording, editing, preserving, transmitting, monitoring, interpreting, and teaching of a purely linguistic corpus -- and the eternal regeneration of the original text, either by simple repetition or by elaboration and commentary. The science of lexicography, it hardly needs saying, was literally fundamental in this process, while the study of pre-Islamic poetry was important in two complementary ways, both in which al-Khalīl was deeply involved. In the first place, poetry was the ultimate lexicographical reference point for the new Islamic vocabulary and the formal linguistic ground from which the "Arab" Qurʾān historically emerged. In the second place, the manifest subtlety, complexity, and beauty of Arabic poetry was a powerful agent in the creation and assertion of Arab cultural identity within the religion that depended so much on the Arabic language but where Arabs were increasingly an ethnic minority. The early scholars may have lacked an explicit scientific program, but they were alive to the need for stabilization and systematization, and they consciously moved towards the establishment of the necessary disciplines from their own intellectual resources. It was not a group of scientists, however, but of pious and respected individuals, including al-Khalīl, who carried authority at the beginning of this endeavor, and it is not only probable but also historically indispensable that their authority should indeed be derived from their piety.

The notion of authority being derived from piety is a central presupposition of this paper. A remarkable feature of Islamic science, unmistakably demonstrated by al-Khalīl, is that a scientific truth acquires its acceptability not from the methods or principles that produced it, but from the personal aura of the individual who enunciated it. This is also the case in Western science,[65] but we mostly delude ourselves that it is the scientific method alone that leads infallibly to final truth, ignoring the fact that as long as every (Western) scientific theory is inevitably replaced by another sooner or later, no theory can be regarded as expressing a final truth. Orthodox medieval Islam (philosophers, Muʿtazilīs, and mystics apart!) avoided that kind of idealism by relegating all such speculations to the fallible domain of human reason and subordinating science and scholarship to a religious truth that lay outside reason. Using the (un-Islamic) position held by al-Fārābī as a convenient antithesis, we might say that whereas the philosopher believed it was enough to apply the method of enquiry correctly to be assured of arriving at the truth, the Muslim scholar started with the truth already and only needed to be completely pious and orthodox for the natural exercise of his human reason to lead inevitably to sound conclusions. As the sciences initiated by al-Khalīl continued to evolve and their importance for the interpretation and administration of Islam to grow, so the personality of their founder proportionately increased in holiness and wisdom until, and it should now not seem like any kind of exaggeration, it was perfectly reasonable to equate him with Aristotle. It was al-Khalīl who said that "the marvels [of creation] draw us towards knowledge and the marvels of knowledge are the pastures of the intellect,"[66] and his inexhaustible urge to ask questions, which is the mark of a genius, has justly evoked the admiration of Western scholars.[67]

Al-Khalīl is thus a paradigm for practically the whole range of activities proper to the Muslim intellectual: He is not only pious far beyond the conventional and completely familiar with the whole Islamic syllabus, but he is also a creative thinker, a shrewd and perspicacious teacher, and a master of Arabic, both linguistically and stylistically combining the attributes of the sage and courtier within the person of a scholar. It is absolutely immaterial whether this figure corresponds to historical reality, since it has become the narrative reality anyway, rather as if a blurred (and therefore meaningless) image has been subjected to an intense and purposeful focusing in order to confirm that Islam offered, as early as the second century A.H. (eighth century A.D.), an environment in which a genius could realize his full potential, even, as al-Khalīl did, embracing the essentials of the "foreign" sciences and thereby giving them a place in

Islam.

Although this paper has not concerned itself with tracing the evolution of the idealized al-Khalīl in a strict historical sequence, it is of the utmost significance to note that the process was under way as early as al-Jāḥiẓ (d. A.H. 255/A.D. 868), Ibn Qutayba (d. A.H. 276/A.D. 889), and al-Mubarrad (d. A.H. 285/A.D. 898). Whatever was added later could only reinforce what was already believed about the man and had to be consistent both with what was genuinely known of him and with the purposes for which the qualities of the saint and scholar accrued around him.[68] By the fourth century A.H. (tenth A.D.), it is likely that this persona had already been long accepted, to judge arbitrarily by a minor work such as the *Mujtanā* of Ibn Durayd (d. A.H. 321/A.D. 933), a wisdom anthology in which al-Khalīl rubs shoulders with an exalted cast of sages from Luqmān to Jesus, as well as the ancient Greeks and Persians.[69]

In conclusion it is probably a good idea to reemphasize the fact that the validity and accuracy of the biographical sources, not to mention the complex literary process by which the portrait of al-Khalīl evolved, have been deliberately disregarded in the present inquiry, though they certainly deserve investigation in some appropriate place. However, what al-Khalīl achieved, he achieved in, through, and for Islam, and this essay has merely tried to argue that from this perspective al-Khalīl, as depicted in the literature, is both a coherent and a necessary figure for the reasons that have been briefly outlined. In this way perhaps some depth may be added to our perception of al-Khalīl beyond regarding him as merely a disembodied scientific pioneer or an intellectual without a personality or a society in which to function. The picture is completed by the account of his death, the perfect exit for an altruistic but absent-minded professor: While trying to devise a way to teach his slave-girl arithmetic so that she would not be cheated in the market, al-Khalīl walks into a column of the mosque, cracks his head against it, and dies.[70] The beauty of the story (and who even needs to believe that it is true?) is that he met his death while exercising his mind in a charitable purpose, like the pious man that he was, which in its way confirms the hypothesis of this paper

Notes

1. F. Rosenthal, *Knowledge Triumphant, the Concept of Knowledge in Medieval Islam* (Leiden, 1970), passim. Note also G. E. von Grunebaum, *Medieval Islam* (Chicago, 1953), 241-50 on the general topic of scholarship and character. The article of R. Sellheim, "Gelehrte und Gelehrsamkeit im Reiche der Chalifen," in E. Kaufmann, ed., *Festgabe für Paul Kirn zum 70. Geburtstag* (Berlin, 1961), 54-79, unfortunately could not be consulted.

2. For convenience only, the earliest source will usually be given in these notes. The great debt to al-Marzubānī (d. A.H. 384/A.D. 994) will become apparent, though we have to rely on the accuracy of the much later version of his *Muqtabas* that survives in the form of the *Mukhtaṣar* of al-Ḥāfiẓ al-Yaghmūrī (d. A.H. 673/A.D. 1274), edited by R. Sellheim (Wiesbaden, 1964). Another version of al-Marzubānī's work, under the title *al-Mukhtār min al-muqtabas*, by 'Alī ibn Ḥasan ibn Mu'āwiya, a contemporary of al-Yaghmūrī, (Sellheim, *Muqtabas*, intro. 16) has been published in facsimile by F. Sezgin, (Frankfurt, 1990), but it adds little to the information given by al-Marzubānī (Sellheim, intro. 18f). However, there are times when the *Mukhtār* contains material not found in the *Mukhtaṣar*, see notes 30, 46, and 56 below.

3. Al-Mubarrad, *Kāmil*, ed. W. Wright (Leipzig, 1868-92), 232.

4. Al-Marzubānī, *Muqtabas*, 56; Yāqūt, *Mu'jam al-udabā'*, ed. D. S. Margliouth (Cairo, 1927), 4:181. E. Bräunlich, "Al-Khalīl und das Kitāb al-'Ain", *Islamica* 2 (1926), 60, makes more or less the same observations on al-Khalīl's piety but from later sources. The alternation of pilgrimage and *ghazw* may well be a conventional eulogy: Hārūn al-Rashīd is praised in the same terms, for example, by Ibn al-Ṭiqṭaqā in *al-Fakhrī*, [*Elfachri, Geschichte der Islamischen Reiche*...] ed. W. Ahlwardt (Gotha, 1860), 230. Abū 'Awn 'Abdullāh b. 'Awn Ibn Artabān was a *mawlā* of 'Abdullāh b. Durra, "a distinguished traditionist and one of Ibn Sīrīn's disciples. He died

A.H. 151 (A.D. 768)", according to Mac Guckin de Slane's translation of Ibn Khallikān, *Wafayāt al-a'yān* (Paris, 1843), 1:587 n. 11. See also Ibn Sa'd, [Ibn Saad], *Biographien*, ed. E. Sachau etc. (Leiden, 1904-40), index.

5. So according to the editor's footnote in *Luma' al-adillah fī uṣūl al-naḥw*, ed. A. Amer (Stockholm, etc., 1963), 35, n. b., referring to al-Suyūṭī, *Muzhir,* ed. M. A. Jād al-Mawlā, et al., (Cairo, n.d.), 1:129 and *Iqtirāḥ* (Hyderabad, 1359), 22-24. In fact in the *Muzhir* al-Suyūṭī is not so specific and merely suggests "such as Abū Zayd, al-Khalīl, al-Aṣma'ī, Abū Ḥātim, Abū 'Ubayda and their sort," and the *Iqtirāḥ* reference is simply to Ibn Jinnī's views on the general conditions for unique transmission and does not mention these four. Al-Khalīl himself was probably too pious to claim this distinction himself, however, cf. Ibn Fāris, *al-Ṣāḥibī fī fiqh al-lugha*, ed. M. Chouémi (Beirut, 1964), 47, who explains that al-Khalīl would never have pretended to an exhaustive knowledge of the whole language as some have imputed to him.

6. Al-Mizzī, Jamāl al-Dīn, *Tahdhīb al-Kamāl fī asmā' al-rijāl* (Beirut, 1987), 8:333; further investigation could of course reveal more activity than al-Mizzī has noted.

7. *Encyclopaedia of Islam* (2d. ed.), art. "al-Khalīl b. Aḥmad" (R. Sellheim).

8. For the dry bread: al-Sīrāfī, *Akhbār al-naḥwiyyīn*, ed. F. Krenkow (Paris, 1936), 38, or al-Marzubānī, *Muqtabas* 67; for the reed hut: Ibn al-Qifṭī, *Inbāh al-ruwāh*, ed. M. A. F. Ibrāhīm (Cairo, 1950-55), 1:345. The bread may well have been made more palatable by the fruits of the orchard he is said to have inherited (R. Sellheim, "al-Khalīl ibn Aḥmad").

9. Al-Ābī, *Nathr al-durr*, ed. 'Uthmān Bū Ghanmī (Tunis, 1983), 126.

10. Al-Marzubānī, *Muqtabas*, 56.

11. This in spite of a disclaimer that he did not compose poetry because "what comes to me I do not like, and what I like will not come to me!", al-Jāḥiẓ, *Ḥayawān*, ed. M. A. S. Hārūn (Cairo, 1969), 3:132. This paper makes no attempt to deal with the sizable number of verses attributed to al-Khalīl.

12. Al-Sīrāfī, *Akhbār al-naḥwiyyīn*, 39:
*wa-qablaka dāwā l-marīḍa l-ṭabību * fa-'āsha l-marīḍu wa-māta l-ṭabību*
*fa-kun musta'iddan li-dā'ī l-fanā'i * fa-'inna lladhī ātin huwa qarību.*

13. Al-Marzubānī, *Muqtabas*, 63:
*wa-māhiya illā laylatun thumma yawmuhā * wa-ḥawlun ilā ḥawlin wa-shahrun ilā shahrin*
*maṭāyā yuqarribna l-jadīda min al-balā * wa-yudnīna l-kirāma min al-qabri*
*wa-yatrukna azwāja l-ghayūri li-ghayrihi * wa-yub'idna juthmāna l-shaḥiḥi min al-wafri.*

14. Ibn 'Abd Rabbih, *al-'Iqd al-farīd*, ed. Aḥmad Amīn, etc. (Cairo, 1926), 2:217, 4:276, where earlier sources are also mentioned, viz., al-Jāḥiẓ, *Bayān*, ed. M. A. S. Hārūn, (Cairo, 1948), 2:98, Ibn Qutayba, *'Uyūn al-akhbār* (Cairo, 1923-30), 2:127, neither of whom actually mentions al-Khalīl in this context, however.

15. Al-Zubaydī, *Ṭabaqāt al-naḥwiyyīn*, ed. M. A. F. Ibrāhīm (Cairo, 1954), 44. "Divine" renders *rabbānī* literally by affinity with the English term for a learned cleric.

16. Al-Zubaydī, *Ṭabaqāt al-naḥwiyyīn*, 44.

17. Al-Marzubānī, *Muqtabas*, 60.

18. Al-Marzubānī, *Muqtabas* 60. Cf. also al-Jāḥiẓ, *Bayān* 1:274, "let your debates with your students be a way of finding out what you do not know."

19. Ibn al-'Imād, *Shadharāt al-dhahab* (Beirut, n.d.), 1:276: *inna l-mujība yufakkiru qabla l-jawābi wa-qabīḥun an yufakkira ba'dahu wa-qāla mā ujību bi-jawābin ḥattā a'rifa mā 'alayya fīhi min al-i'tirāḍāti wa-l-mu'ākhadhāti.*

20. J. van Ess, "Disputationspraxis in der islamischen Theologie," *Revue des Études Islamiques* 44 (1976), reissued in *L'enseignement en Islam et en occident au moyen âge*, ed. D. Sourdel, J. Sourdel-Thomine (Paris, 1977).

21. Ibn Abī 'Awn, *al-Ajwiba l-muskita*, 25 (130): *inna l-mujība idhā btada'a bi-l-jawābi qabuḥa bihi an yufakkira* (see also note 24). This version is also supported by the *Mukhtār* (see note 2) 136.

22. See the introduction to the edition of the *Ajwiba*, 119f.

23. We know from Ibn Abī 'Awn's own introduction, *al-Ajwiba l-muskita*, 1 and 3, that part of the technique of answering questions was to avoid *ibtidā'āt* ("declarative statements," the same term as used by al-Khalīl,) which expose the answerer to further questions.

24. There is probably a connection between answering with silence as here and the notion of *ṭalab al-mafqūd* "seeking what is not there," a commonplace both of Ṣūfism and Greek asceticism, e.g. in D. Gutas, *Greek*

Wisdom Literature in Arabic Translation (Newhaven, 1975), 62, and cf. al-Kindī, "Every desired thing, external to us, is not present (i.e., available) when wanted, nor any desired thing can be called present when it is lost," translation by A. S. Bazmee Ansari in George N. Atiyeh, *Al-Kindi: the Philosopher of the Arabs* (Rawalpindi, 1966), 246 (Arabic text, 226: *laysa kullu maṭlūbin khārijin ʿannā bi-mawjūdin kullamā ṭuliba wa-lā mawjūdun minhu ʿaqība shayʾin matā fuqida*). This must also be the sense of al-Khalīl's enigmatic definition of the ascetic (*zāhid*) as one who "does not seek what he lacks until what he has is gone," *lā yaṭlubu l-mafqūda ḥattā yadhhaba l-mawjūdu*, Ibn Abī ʿAwn, *al-Ajwiba l-muskita*, ed. M. A. Yousef (Berlin, 1988), 87 (514); a slightly different version in al-Marzubānī, *al-Muqtabas*, 63: *ḥattā yafqida l-mawjūdu.* Al-Ghazālī seems to be saying much the same in *al-Munqidh min al-ḍalāl*, ed.and trans. by F. Jabre (Beirut, 1969), Arabic text, 14: "The point of all these stories [of my search for truth] is that the search should always be conducted with the utmost earnestness, *to the point of seeking what should not be sought. A priori* facts should not have to be sought for they are at hand, and what is at hand will vanish and be lost when it is sought, but if you seek what should not be sought you can never be accused of falling short in the search." Jabre's French translation (66) reproduces this paradox fairly well, though with apparent misgivings, while Watt's version literally demystifies the whole procedure by translating the key clause as "up to the stage of seeking what is not sought (but stops short of that)," W. M. Watt, *The Faith and Practice of al-Ghazālī* (London, 1953), 26. Since al-Ghazālī was a thorough Sufi when he wrote those words, we should not expect them to have such a banal meaning as Watt gives them.

Another example is found below (see note 43), while the debate with Abū Shamir (see notes 55f) touches upon a related issue, from a quite different perspective.

25. In this incident al-Maʾmūn's curiosity is presumably genuine, though it is clear that Aristotle wished to terminate the conversation! See Ibn al-Nadīm, *Fihrist*, ed. G. Flügel (Leipzig, 1871-2, repr. Beirut 1964), 243 and Ibn Abī Uṣaybiʿa, *ʿUyūn al-anbāʾ*, ed. A. Müller (Cairo, 1882), 186.

26. Ḥunayn ibn Isḥāq was once sent away for the same reason, as reported in M. W. Dols, *Medieval Islamic Medicine* (Berkeley, etc., 1984), 7, though no sources are given.

27. Ibn al-ʿImād, *Shadharāt al-dhabab*, (Beirut, n.d.), 1:275. A.H. 1080/A.D. 1670 is the date of the work's composition.

28. Ibn al- ʻImād, *Shadharāt al-dhahab*, 1:276 gives the fullest and most satisfying version of this incident. The verse runs: *idhā lam tastaṭiʻ shayʼan fa-daʻhu * wa jāwizhu ilā mā tastaṭīʻu.*

29. *Ṭabaqāt al-naḥwiyyīn,* 45, though not every biographer is as explicit as al-Zubaydī, and the scepticism of Bräunlich, *Islamica* 2 (1926), 62, is fully justified. In particular the absence of information about the circumstances and contents of the meeting arouses suspicion.

30. E.g., *Risāla fī l-faḍl bayn al-ʻadāwa wa-l-ḥasad*, ed. M. A. S. Hārūn (Cairo, 1964), 1:350, quoted by Ṭ. al-Ḥājirī in his introduction to the *Bukhalāʼ*(Cairo, 1981), 41. For further references see C. Pellat, *Le milieu basrien et la formation d'al-Ǧāḥiẓ* (Paris, 1953), 62, who unfortunately gives no details of the "remarks on Ibn al-Muqaffaʻ and al-Jāḥiẓ," which he found in a *Risāla fī l-muʻallimīn* in the margin of the Cairo edition of al-Mubarrad, *Kāmil*, 32-33. He also refers to H. Hirschfeld, "A volume of essays by al-Jāḥiẓ" in T. W. Arnold, R. A. Nicholson, eds. *A Volume of Oriental Studies presented to Edwarde G. Browne* (Cambridge, 1922), who makes the fascinating assertion on page 207 that al-Jāḥiẓ regarded both al-Khalīl and Ibn al-Muqaffaʻ as "incompetent in matters educational," probably paraphrasing al-Jāḥiẓ's own criticism of al-Khalīl that he made the mistake of exceeding his competence by writing books on topics outside his field, *Ḥayawān*, 1:150. It is interesting, too, that this criticism of al-Khalīl by al-Jāḥiẓ is alluded to in the *Mukhtār*, 185, but not in the *Muqtabas*, both ostensibly abridgments of the same work (see note 2).

31. Al-Marzubānī, *Muqtabas*, 61.

32. Ibn al-Qifṭī, *Taʼrīkh al-ḥukamāʼ*, ed. J. Lippert (Leipzig, 1903), 171. To repeat, historical veracity is not the question here: the fact that al-Khalīl died before Ḥunayn was born is less important than the obviously felt need to bring them together.

33. Al-Zubaydī, *Ṭabaqāt al-naḥwiyyīn*, 47.

34. Al-Azharī, *Tahdhīb al-lugha*, ed. M. A. S. Hārūn, (Cairo, 1964-7), 14:259, s.v. *batta*. I am grateful to C. H. M. Versteegh for bringing this information to my attention.

35. Al-Marzubānī, *Muqtabas*, 63.

36. Al-Marzubānī, *Muqtabas*, 65. The Qadarī maintains that a predetermined action cannot proceed both from himself and from God, and the rebuttal is a sophism, of course, based on a grammatical rather than an ontological distinction.

37. Al-Marzubānī, *Muqtabas*, 69. Other interpretations are possible: it could be a pro-Muʻtazilī story demonstrating a mastery of

Arabic which was a prerequisite for admission into debates with the orthodox.

38. Al-Marzubānī, *Muqtabas*, 65.

39. Ibn Qutayba, *'Uyūn al-akhbār*, 3:12. In al-Marzubānī, *Muqtabas*, 61, al-Khalīl expresses the same idea in metrical form, though not in the same context. The incident reflects the concern that every participant in a *majlis* should be comfortably and adequately seated, about which there are several *Ḥadīth*s.

40. Al-Marzubānī, *Muqtabas*, 63:

*wa-mā shay'un aḥabba ilā la'īmin * idhā sabba l-kirāma min al-jawābi*
*mutārakatu l-la'īmi bilā jawābin * ashaddu 'alā l-la'īmi min al-sabābi.*

41. Al-Marzubānī, *Muqtabas*, 59:

*ṣif khalqa khawdin ka-mithli l-shamsi idh bazaghat **
yaḥẓā l-ḍajī'u bihā najlā'a mi'ṭāri.

"Describe a maid's exquisite charms, like the sun when zenithwards: the lover sleeping in her arms she, wide-eyed, fragrant joy affords!"

42. Ibn Qutayba, *'Uyūn al-akhbār*, II, 160.

43. Al-Sīrāfī, *Akhbār al-naḥwiyyīn*, 39, quotes the poem alone:

*law kunta ta'lamu mā aqūlu 'adhartanī * aw kuntu ajhalu mā taqūlu 'adhaltuka*
*lākin jahilta maqālatī fa-'adhaltanī * wa-'alimtu annaka jāhulun fa-'adhartuka*

but the earliest account of the context appears to be in *al-Muqtabas*, 58, the famous incident where al-Khalīl hears the coppersmith hammering on his trays and he conceives the idea of the poetic meters.

The poem relies on a multiple antithesis of *'ilm* and *jahl*, and of puns on *i'tadhara* and *i'tadhala*, and the translation tries to reproduce at least the spirit of the wordplay. In Ibn 'Abd Rabbih, *al-'Iqd al-farīd* 2:223, a completely different account is given of the occasion of the poem: This time al-Khalīl has been rebuked by Kaysān for not only spending too long thinking up a reply to Kaysān's question but worse, producing an incomprehensible answer! The echo of the incident described above (see notes 19ff) is too strong to be ignored: both there and here the issue is the relationship between question and answer, speech and silence, matters of deep concern in the etiquette of the *majlis* and the interaction between master and pupil.

44. Ibn 'Abd Rabbih, *al-'Iqd al-farīd*, 4:190. "Extremities" here clearly refers to the beginning and end of an utterance, whether in prose or verse, and the formula recalls the proverb *khayru l-kalām mā qalla wa-dalla*, though other interpretations are possible, to be sure.

45. Al-Marzubānī, *Muqtabas*, 67. "Break down" translates *yanqaṭi'a*, lit. stop speaking and be unable to go on, the pedagogue's nightmare (cf. al-Ghazālī's spiritual crisis in 488/1095).

46. Al-Tha'ālibī, *Thimār al-qulūb*, ed. M. A. F. Ibrāhīm (Cairo, 1965), 170. In Abū l-Ṭayyib al-Lughawī, *Marātib al-naḥwiyyīn*, ed. A. F. Ibrāhīm (Cairo, 1955), 38, the foursome is Abū Ḥanīfa, al-Khalīl, Ibn al-Muqaffa', and al-Fazārī, to which list Abū l-Ṭayyib adds al-Jāḥiẓ and al-Kindī, all geniuses, evidently, though in what fields is left for the reader to supply. Cf. also Ḥamza al-Iṣfahānī, *al-Tanbīh fī ḥudūth al-taṣḥīf*, ed. M. A. Ṭalas (Damascus, 1968), 124f. The same story is found in the *Mukhtār* of 'Alī ibn Ḥasan ibn Mu'āwiya, 131, but not in al-Yaghmūrī's *al-Muqtabas* (see note 2).

47. Al-Sīrāfī, *Akhbār al-naḥwiyyīn*, 38.

48. Al-Mubarrad, *Kāmil*, 171.

49. Al-Tha'ālibī, *Thimār al-qulūb*, 323.

50. Al-Marzubānī, *Muqtabas*, 61. Using ± knowledge as the criterion, this series exhausts the possibilities with + +, + -, - + and - - respectively. The Pythagorean echoes in this scheme cannot be overlooked, and it adds considerable piquancy that al-Khalīl was led to discover the Arabic meters by the sound of banging on a metal tray (al-Marzubānī, *Muqtabas,* 58) very much as Pythagoras was inspired to construct his theory of musical intervals by the hammering of a blacksmith upon his anvil, B. Farrington, *Greek Science, Its Meaning for Us* (London, 1961), 50.

51. Al-Marzubānī, *Muqtabas*, 60.

52. Ibn al-Qifṭī, *Inbāh al-ruwāh*, 1:346.

53. There is not a little irony in the fact that al-Fārābī, too, was regarded as a "second Aristotle."

54. Ibn 'Abd Rabbih, *al-'Iqd al-farīd*, 2:213. The episode is also connected with Abū l-Aswad al-Du'alī, cf. Rosenthal, *Knowledge Triumphant*, 258 and 328 n. 3.

55. On this person see J. van Ess, *Theologie und Gesellschaft im 2. und 3. Jahrhundert Hidschra* (Berlin, 1992) 2:174-80. Abū Shamir is described with some affection and respect by al-Jāḥiẓ, *Bayān*, 1:91-2, *Ḥayawān,* 3:357 and note. The story is also in al-Jāḥiẓ, *Hayawān,* 1:37 and Ḥamza al-Iṣfahānī, *al-Tanbīh fī ḥudūth al-taṣḥīf*, ed. M. A. Ṭalas (Damascus, 1968), 121f. Other sources name different participants in the dispute, not always with al-Khalīl as one of them, e.g., Ibn 'Abd al-Barr,

Bahjat al-majālis, ed. M. Mursī, etc. (Cairo, 1962), 1:67.

Is it perhaps going too far to suppose that the kernel of Abū Shamir's retort is the logical necessity of nonexistence (*al-'adam*) in order to define existence, a well-known Mu'tazilite position? Cf. also the remarks in note 24 above.

56. Ibn Abī 'Awn, *al-Ajwiba l-muskita*, 151 (906), and cf. al-Jāḥiẓ, *Ḥayawān,* 1:37, Ibn 'Abd al-Barr, *Bahjat al-majālis,* 1:67. The story is also in the *Mukhtār,* 147, but not in the *Muqtabas* (see note 2).

57. Ibn 'Abd Rabbih, *al-'Iqd al-farīd*, 3:23.

58. Al-Marzubānī, *Muqtabas*, 61:

*i'mal bi-'ilmī wa-in qaṣartu fī 'amalī * yanfa'ka 'ilmī wa-lā yaḍrurka taqṣīrī*

*wa-anẓur li-nafsika fīmā anta fā'iluhu * min al-umūri wa-shammir fawqa tashmīrī*

Not all sources quote the second line. See Rosenthal, *Knowledge Triumphant*, 259 for another translation.

59. Al-Zubaydī, *Ṭabaqāt al-naḥwiyyīn*, 44; a second phrase is also found, "but ignorance conceals the lapse of a fool," *wa-zallatu l-jāhili yukhfīhā l-jahlu*, cf. al-Maydānī, *Majma' al-amthāl*, ed. M. A. F. Ibrāhīm (Cairo, 1977), 2:90.

60. Ibn al-Qifṭī, *Inbāh al-ruwāh*, 1:347. Among other less than positive reflections of al-Khalīl's character is his confession of his enduring shame at having behaved rudely towards al-Farazdaq, al-Marzubānī, *Muqtabas*, 69.

61. Al-Zajjājī, *Majālis al-'ulamā'*, ed. M. A. S. Hārūn (Kuwayt, 1962), 258.

62. Notwithstanding some doubts about his exact contribution to the writing of the *Kitāb al-'ayn* or to Sībawayhi's grammar.

63. The others were Yūnus ibn Ḥabīb, al-Aṣma'ī and Abū 'Amr ibn al-'Alā', according to al-Mizzī, *Tahdhīb al-kamāl*, 8:329; Bräunlich, *Islamica* 2 (1926), 60, has the same list but from a different source.

64. The account of the reasons for the names of the various meters is of dubious value in understanding why they were so called, al-Marzubānī, *al-Muqtabas*, 71.

65. Cf. *Science as a Process: an Evolutionary Account of the Social and Conceptual Development of Science* (Chicago and London, 1988), 31f, where the author, David L. Hull, argues that, although the qualities of "political infighting, the name-calling, parody and ridicule, the arrogance, elitism and use of raw power" are not exclusive to scientists, nevertheless he believes firmly that "some of the behaviour that appears to be most improper actually facilitates the manifest goals of science," and that "the least productive scientists tend to behave most admirably, while those who make the greatest contributions just as frequently behave the most deplorably." We may contrast this with the Greek attitude to scientific morals neatly summarized by E. Itkonen, *Universal History of Linguistics* (Amsterdam & Philadelphia, 1991), 342, that a Stoic and probably most "Eastern" thinkers would have regarded the sentence "A good physicist cannot commit murder" as true. Al-Khalīl, obviously, represents the Greek rather than the contemporary Western ideal!

66. Al-Zubaydī, *Ṭabaqāt al-naḥwiyyīn*, 44.

67. Bräunlich, *Islamica* 2 (1926), 61 has already remarked that "what we can still admire today in al-Khalīl is the brilliance of his mind, with which in hundreds of individual cases he demonstrates the possibility of asking a question." The present paper in fact adds only details to the core of al-Khalīl's personality as it is perceptively summarized by Bräunlich but goes further by suggesting possible reasons for this impression of him that the sources give us.

68. Two extremely favourable references to ʻAlī by al-Khalīl have not been taken into consideration here, but clearly need to be accounted for, viz., Ibn ʻAbd al-Barr, *Bahjat al-majālis* (Cairo, 1962) 1:65 and al-Marzubānī, *Muqtabas*, 57.

69. Ed. M. A. M. Khan (Hyderabad, 1963).

70. Ibn al-Qifṭī, *Inbāh al-ruwāh,* 1:346.

Kitāb al-ʿayn and *Jamharat al-lugha*

Ramzi Baalbaki

The earliest reference to the relations between *Kitāb al-ʿayn* by al-Khalīl ibn Aḥmad (d. A.H. 170/A.D. 786) and *Jamharat al-lugha* by Ibn Durayd (d. A.H. 321/A.D. 933) was, unfortunately, the result of bias and animosity. This occurs in Nifṭawayhi's (d. A.H. 323/A.D. 934) famous lines in which he accused Ibn Durayd of plagiarizing *al-ʿAyn*. In one of these lines, Nifṭawayhi bluntly states that *al-Jamhara* is a modified version of *al-ʿAyn*, the alleged modification being no more than a coverup for plagiarism (*wa-hwa kitābu l-ʿayni illā annahū qad ghayyarah*).[1] The anecdote would have been just another instance of rivalry between ancient Arab scholars were it not for its repeated occurrence in the sources, which is due in part to Ibn Durayd's shrewd rebuttal.[2] Consequently, a conviction seems to have developed in some of the ancient sources that Ibn Durayd had indeed "raided" *al-ʿAyn* and modified its material into the form of a new lexicon.

More surprising, however, is that some contemporary authors accept Nifṭawayhi's claim as true and do not even hesitate to judge *al-Jamhara* in its light. For example, A.M. Shākir asserts that *al-Jamhara* is "extracted" (*muqtabas*) from *al-ʿAyn* or is the same book but in modified form.[3] Similarly, M.A. Abū al-Faraj asserts that Nifṭawayhi's satire argues for the habit of imitation (*taqlīd*) in Arab lexicographical works.[4]

It should be noted, however, that some authors, like Suyūṭī (d.

A.H. 911/A.D. 1505), defended Ibn Durayd and dismissed Niftawayhi's accusation as peer pressure which is not trustworthy in *'ilm al-ḥadīth* (prophetic tradition). In Suyūṭī's words: *kalām al-aqrān fī ba'ḍihim lā yaqdaḥ* (peer testimony does not slander).[5] Among contemporary authors, Naṣṣār challenges the allegation of plagiarism and furnishes, for the very first time, evidence from the text of both lexicons in support of his argument.[6] Despite Naṣṣār's attempt, the relation between *al-'Ayn* and *al-Jamhara* is still far from clear, and further study is warranted by the recent publication of the whole text of the first and of the new edition of the second. It is thus now possible to compare Ibn Durayd's quotations from al-Khalīl with the actual text of *al-'Ayn*, and to compare the use of *shawāhid* (the bulk of attested usage) in each since the present author, in his edition of *al-Jamhara*, indicated the sources of every *shāhid*, with *al-'Ayn* as a basic reference. Here, every common *shāhid* is indicated in the footnotes.

The purpose of this paper is to present a brief outline of the points which prove that the two works are not merely different, but truly disparate or even conflicting in aim, content, and method. But since a detailed comparison, especially in content, would extend far beyond the scope of this paper and would require extremely lengthy quotations, we will content ourselves with a broad outline, the details of which will have to be minimized. The basic points under discussion will include the aim and scope of each lexicon, the organization and coherence, the alphabetical arrangement, the direct references to al-Khalīl by Ibn Durayd, and to a lesser extent, the *shawāhid* and the internal arrangement and exposition of the entries.

The obvious point that seems to have escaped ancient and contemporary scholars alike is the fact that al-Khalīl and Ibn Durayd were each aiming at a different target. In other words, their points of departure are different, and this had its impact on the nature of their work. Al-Khalīl was a genuine innovator, as his works on metrics, grammatical *ʿilla* (causation), and phonetics clearly demonstrate. But whereas his concern for establishing a solid base for grammatical study can best be shown in the terminology he introduced, as hardly any term used by Sībawayhi (d. A.H. 180/A.D. 796) fails to appear in his quotations from al-Khalīl,[7] it is his attempt at discovering the boundaries of linguistic material that is the most manifest proof of his lexicographical insight. First, he determined that the letters of the alphabet, which have a fixed number -- twenty-nine in all, since he differentiated between the *hamza* (glottal stop) and the "soft" *alif* (*al-alif al-layyina*[8]) -- should be subjected to some sort of arrangement, for which he chose the points of articulation. Second, the number of consonant radicals in an Arabic word stem varies from two to five,[9] and the words are thus fixed in that respect, even if they differ in being *ṣaḥīḥ* (sound), *muʿtall* (defective), or *lafīf* (containing two weak radicals). The third principle becomes readily apparent, as the fixed phonemic inventory and number of radicals per word implies that Arabic lexical roots can be manipulated by the inversion of the order of their constituents. Hence al-Khalīl's permutations of consonant ordering within roots which, theoretically at least, yield two sets in biliteral roots, six sets in the triliteral, twenty-four sets in the quadriliteral, and one hundred twenty-four sets in the quinqueliteral.

In the case of Ibn Durayd, and indeed of all Arabic lexicographers after Khalīl, the discovery stage was over: the system whereby all lexical roots can be calculated without exception had already been established. What remained was the improvement or, to use a more neutral word, the modification from within, as in the alphabetical order, the internal arrangement of the entries and their *shawāhid*.

At any rate, the first two sets of fixed elements discovered by al-Khalīl could not be eliminated, as that would have undermined the entire system. Later authors such as Jawharī (A.H. 393/A.D. 1002) had to abolish the third principle in order to nullify the second. In other words, if the permutations are discarded, a substitute method for consonant sequence and root length has to be found in order to arrange entries. In the light of this, we should understand the fact that Ibn Durayd endorsed al-Khalīl's three principles, but modified each of them to suit his own ideas. He introduced three basic modifications as follows:

(1) As to the first concept namely, the arrangement of the letters of the alphabet, Ibn Durayd chose a completely different system, that of the "normal" alphabetical order (*alif, bāʾ, tāʾ, thāʾ*, etc.). His assertion that "the man in the street's knowledge of this, like that of the specialist and the student, is free from confusion and able to grasp what is intended"[10] is a courteous way of saying that al-Khalīl's arrangement of the letters cannot be maintained. Indeed, as Haywood notes, al-Khalīl's "novel alphabet" had nothing in its favor but the fact that "it drew attention to phonetic laws, and offered means of detecting foreign words"[11] -- points, it must be noted, not normally considered part of a lexicographer's job.

(2) In the second concept, Ibn Durayd adheres to the division described by al-Khalīl, whereby the number of radicals in an Arabic lexical root varies from a minimum of two to a maximum of five, but elaborates this division to include more subdivisions,[12] such as the hamzated triliteral roots, their *lafīf* (containing two weak radicals) and *maqṣūr* (ending with ā, i.e., *alif maqṣūra*) forms, and the quadriliteral roots formed by reduplication of a hamzated base.[13] Unfortunately, the facilitation that resulted from Ibn Durayd's rejection of the arrangement of Arabic phonemes/letters according to their points of articulation was more than offset by this elaborated division, which made *al-Jamhara* probably the most difficult Arabic lexicon to consult without the aid of indexes -- i.e., without its rearrangement!

(3) The case of the third principle is different. Here, Ierdfsxc bn Durayd could not make any modifications in a matter of mathematical nature, the permutations being the product of straightforward calculation. However, the matter is more complex, and it is the interrelation with (1) and (2) above that is crucial. The change Ibn Durayd introduced was the arrangement of his lexicon according to root length, whereby the different permutations are a function first of the form and then of its constituent phonemes.

This is an obvious departure from al-Khalīl's method of listing all the possible root permutations under each letter/phoneme, arranged by root length within the chapter on each letter. The implication of this is far-reaching, as it shows that al-Khalīl's work is the result of a rigorous application of the principles involved in his three fixed concepts. This rigor is an essential feature of discovery based on a system that must be strictly applied, while Ibn Durayd allowed himself much more room for manoeuvre and could afford to emcompass the morphological panorama of the language, since he was not absorbed in the constant effort of exhausting the roots according to a system he was continuously bound to be conscious of and observe.

The extent of Ibn Durayd's departure from al-Khalīl -- so extensively ignored by ancient and contemporary scholars -- regarding the three above-mentioned concepts becomes more meaningful when one traces its impact on the nature of the contents of both lexicons. Here lies further proof of the salient differences between the two works, possibly of wider significance than the points discussed above. The following three points illustrate this:

(1) *Al-ʿAyn* is much more organized and systematic than *al-Jamhara*. In *al-ʿAyn*, each root occupies a single entry; that is, it occurs only once and is not repeated elsewhere in the lexicon. This seems the logical outcome of al-Khalīl's application of his three principles and in line with his mathematical approach (especially

evident in the permutations) which dictates a one-to-one relationship between the root and its position within a strictly hierarchically arranged system. The reoccurence of roots in different locations in the lexicon would have contrasted sharply with Khalīl's efforts at systematization and defeated his purpose of providing entries for roots within the exact slots dictated by the root consonant permutations.

On the other hand, *al-Jamhara* scarcely satisfies the organization requirements expected in a lexicon. Particularly remarkable is the recurrence of one root in different places of the lexicon. This does not only apply to those roots discussed as part of the author's commentary on the *shawāhid* [14] -- this being a common practice in almost all Arabic lexicons -- but roots for which more than one actual entry is assigned. For example, the root ʾ *by* is handled under the weak biliteral roots (229), the roots appended to the sound triliterals; i.e., *b-w-w-ʾ-y* (1029) and *b-y-w-ʾ-y* (1030), and the *nawādir* (rare usage) of *hamz* (1090). Moreover, it appears in four other disparate places: under the section of *faʿala* and *afʿala* (1266), under the *lughāt* (attested usage) attributed to Abū Zayd (d. A.H. 215/A.D. 830) (1306; 1307), and under the plurals of the different patterns (1337).[15] Similarly, *rwy*[16] and *ṣb*ʾ [17] each appear in nine different places.[18] Indeed, the whole chapter entitled: "*abwāb mā laḥiqa bi-l-thulāthī l-ṣaḥīḥ bi-ḥarf min ḥurūf al-līn wa mā tashaʿʿaba minhu*" (chapters on roots appended to the sound triliterals by a weak letter and related roots) (1016-85) is largely composed of material that had already been covered either in *bāb al-thunāʾī l-ṣaḥīḥ* (chapter on sound biliterals) (53-172) or in *bāb al-thunāʾī fī l-muʿtall* (chapter on defective biliterals) (229-51).[19]

Another remarkable feature of the poor organization in *al-Jamhara* is the inclusion under *thulāthī* of some biliteral words with the feminine ending *h*, such as *ṣuffa* (hall), and the inclusion under *rubāʿī* of some triliteral roots also with the feminine ending, such as *qirba* (bottle) and *jaḥma* (eye). This, however, is not due to Ibn Durayd's ignorance of morphology as Ibn Jinnī (d. A.H. 392/A.D. 1001),[20] would have us believe, since he was aware of that discrepancy and explained it by the fact that these words have no masculine, and so the feminine ending is like an entity inseparable from the word (*ka-l-ḥarf al-lāzim*).[21] This treatment of the feminine ending is by no means a standard practice of his, however, and thus confusion becomes more prevalent.[22]

It would be too simplistic to content oneself with the above "abnormalities" and explain them away as mere examples of Ibn Durayd's disorganized plan. Indeed, Haywood notes that *al-Jamhara* is "the most confused Arab dictionary ever written,"[23] but fails to produce any explanation. For his part, Naṣṣār expresses his wonder at why *al-ʿAyn* includes a number of important features which *al-Jamhara* lacks, despite the fact that the former, historically speaking, precedes the latter.[24] As for the specific question of the feminine suffix, Krenkow suggests that the reason why Ibn Durayd treats it as if it were a radical, and places words that end with it in accordance with that, is to help the ignorant reader find these words, since a beginner would probably think that the suffix is part of the root![25]

Aḥmad Fāris al-Shidyāq seems to be the only author who tries to provide a general explanation for the contrast between the two works; he blames Ibn Durayd's failures on the method of *imlāʾ* (dictation) which, he says, is acceptable in literature but not in language.[26] The correct explanation, however, is of a much more substantial nature and is in harmony with our line of argument presented above.[27] The two works are the result and embodiment of their authors' concerns and aims. In *al-ʿAyn* the entry of a root in, and only in, its logical position within the system reflects al-Khalīl's efforts as a discoverer, who is necessarily an organizer. The confusion in *al-Jamhara* reflects the position of an author untroubled by the responsibility of discovery and unburdened by its inherent corollary of organized presentation. Putting that aside, his effort was directed at the advancement of explanations, exhaustive use of the *shawāhid,* and accumulation of material from various sources, as we shall see in (2) below.

(2) The content of *al-'Ayn* is coherent, in the sense that it includes a well-defined body of material that satisfies the author's aim of assembling linguistic data according to an elaborate plan. Thus *al-'Ayn* ends where it is expected to end, and the exhaustion of the entries brings it to its logical conclusion with the fulfillment of its purpose.

In contrast, *al-Jamhara* lacks this coherence, and does not end with the exhaustion of lexical roots. Following the section on quinqueliterals, supposed to have been the last according to the major divisions of the work, is a multitude of short chapters that together form a body of material alien to the rest of the lexicon, not as far as content is concerned, but mainly in respect to the principle of arrangement involved. These include chapters on certain patterns, dialectal features, *nawādir* (rare usage), loan-words, plurals, and words particular to pre-Islamic usage or to certain technical subjects such as swords, spearheads, and arrows.[28] Here again, simplistic explanations are unconvincing, as is the suggestion that "some later hand put together a number of Ibn Durayd's lexicographical works and forged the introduction."[29] This is contradicted by the fact that Ibn Durayd's departure from adhering to the principle of presenting only roots as entries is already apparent in his section on quadriliterals and quinqueliterals.[30] In part of the former and all of the latter, the form and not the root is the criterion, as is the case in most of the final parts of the lexicon, referred to by Haywood as a "bewildering series of short chapters ...dealing mostly with word-forms." Moreover, these chapters precede the epilogue which seems to conclude the whole work.

The main issue here is the difference in arrangement between those short chapters -- and the section on quinqueliterals and part of the section on quadriliterals -- and the rest of the lexicon. It should be remembered that each arrangement serves a different purpose. Ibn Sīda's (d. A.H. 458/A.D. 1066) case, in this respect, is of particular significance. As late as the middle of the fifth century A.H., this author saw the need for maintaining both kinds of arrangement, though in separate works. He clearly marks the difference between the root-arranged lexicon, which he calls *mujannas* (classified), as embodied in his *al-muḥkam*, and the subject-arranged lexicon, i.e., *ghayr mujannas* (unclassified), as is his *al-mukhaṣṣaṣ*.[31] This provides the clue for the answer: Ibn Durayd, confident that the exhaustion aspect was taken care of by al-Khalīl's principles, was more concerned with elucidating the material and exhausting it from more than one direction. He was aware that the first kind of arrangement, according to which most of *al-Jamhara* is written, helps the reader who knows that the word exists but wants to check its meaning, while the other kind of arrangement, mainly according to form, provides the reader with a list of words of a pattern he may want to learn about or with a subject the relevant vocabulary of which he may want to check, as in the case of swords, spearheads, arrows, etc.

(3) The introduction of *al-'Ayn* is a basic part of the lexicon, as it explains the principles upon which al-Khalīl bases his work. Thus, his discussion of the points of articulation corresponds directly to the order of letters in the text, and his determination of the number of radicals in Arabic roots corresponds directly to the internal arrangement of items within the chapter on each letter. Similarly, al-Khalīl's concern in his introduction for some of the phonetic characteristics and phonotactics of Arabic words (e.g., that no Arabic quadriliteral or quinqueliteral root can be devoid of liquids or labials[32] and that no Arabic word begins with *n-r*)[33] is linked to his plan of

exhaustively listing all potential Arabic roots, explaining what is in actual usage, and pointing out what is only theoretically possible. This introduction is possibly the most explicit proof of al-Khalīl's originality and of the largely indigenous origins of Arabic lexicography.

By contrast, the introduction of *al-Jamhara* bears no such relationship to the lexicon itself. In particular, it looks odd that Ibn Durayd discusses in his introduction the characteristics (*ṣifāt)* of sounds and their points of articulation, when this has no bearing at all on his arrangement of the letters according to the *alif, bā', tā', thā'* system. As for the other parts of the introduction, namely, the discussion of the number of radicals in Arabic words and of some phonetic characteristics of these words, although they are echoed in the lexicon itself, which is arranged according to root length and supposedly includes Arabic roots only, their inclusion in the introduction is a tribute by the author to al-Khalīl and is definitely not intended to put forward to the reader the theoretical basis on which the work rests. In short, nowhere more than in its introduction do we find *al-Jamhara* so similar to *al-ʻAyn* in content and yet so drastically different from it in significance and purport.

Another approach for examining the relationship between *al-ʻAyn* and *al-Jamhara* is to analyze the references made by Ibn Durayd to al-Khalīl --- an exercise made possible by the publication of the whole of *al-ʻAyn.* According to the indexes of the new edition of *al-Jamhara,* al-Khalīl is mentioned sixty-seven times,[34] and although *al-ʻAyn* is specifically mentioned only three times,[35] reference to al-Khalīl is merely reference to his lexicon. We shall examine some of the references to al-Khalīl by Ibn Durayd in order to be able to determine more specifically the nature of the latter's view of his predecessor. To the exclusion of the instances in which Ibn Durayd rightly quotes al-Khalīl or makes use of his *shawāhid*, the following points of special significance for the discussion will be mentioned:

(a) Ibn Durayd reports al-Khalīl's claim that *sha'waẓa* (prestidigitation) is not an Arabic word and then expresses his doubts about its correctness.[36] Exactly the opposite is found in *al-'Ayn* where al-Khalīl not only says that *sha'waẓiyy* is an Arabic word, but also describes it as a literary word (*kalima 'āliya*).[37]

(b) He attributes to al-Khalīl and Abū Mālik (second century A.H./ eighth century A.D.) that *shiwā' ma'lūs* refers to the *shiwā'* eaten with *samn*,[38] and that *'alas* means *shiwā' masmūn* (roasted meat), that is, containing *samn*.[39] The text of *al-'Ayn* is different. There we find the following statement: "*wa-l-'als: al-shiwā' al-samīn*,"[40] with *'als* and not *'alas*, and with *samīn* (fat) referring to the animal[41] and not *masmūn* (cooked or eaten with fat). It could be that Ibn Durayd, in relying on memory, mixed up the two meanings of the root *smn*, and substituted one for the other.[42]

(c) He rejects al-Khalīl's contention that the word *'adas* used in restraining mules is taken from the proper noun *'adas*, a man at the time of Sulaymān ibn Dāwūd, famous for his harshness with mules.[43] Indeed, the text of *al-'Ayn* confirms this contention, although slightly differently, as *ḥadas* are said to have been muleteers in the days of Sulaymān.[44]

(d) He also rejects al-Khalīl's allegation that *'amṣ* is a kind of food, and says that he does not know what it is.[45] Under the root *'-m-ṣ*,[46] al-Khalīl says that *'āmiṣ* and *'ā'āmiṣ* mean *khāmīz*, a kind of food.

(e) He blames Layth ibn Muẓaffar (a contemporary of al-Khalīl), and not al-Khalīl, for a mistake that occurred in the chapter of *sīn* in *al-'Ayn*, namely, that *sadaf* is a synonym for *shadaf* (person, figure).[47] However, nothing is mentioned in either entry in *al-'Ayn* concerning this synonymity.[48]

(f) He dismisses the attribution to al-Khalīl of the usage: *yawm bughāth* (the battle of Bugāth), saying that it is *yawm bu'āth*.[49]

Indeed, *bughāth* occurs in *b-gh-th*,[50] but *bu'āth* does not in *b-'-th*.[51] Reference here is most probably made to Layth, and this is supported by the fact that Ibn Manẓūr (d. A.H. 711/A.D. 1311), on the authority of Azharī (d. A.H. 370/A.D. 980), blames Layth for this glaring mistake which, he says, al-Khalīl would not possibly have made.[52]

(g) He denies knowledge of the nature of the drink called *fuqqā'* and of its etymology.[53] No reference is made here to al-Khalīl, who not only explains in his lexicon that this is a drink made of barley, but also proposes an etymology for it saying that it was called so due to the foam on top.[54]

(h) In the entry *k-b-'*,[55] he attributes to al-Khalīl that *kab'* means *man'*, and gives no other meaning for the word. In *al-'Ayn*, however, al-Khalīl does not mention this meaning, but actually mentions another meaning (examining and weighing coins)[56] which itself is lacking in *al-Jamhara*!

(i) He mentions that *ṭa's* is a euphemism for *nikāḥ* (intercourse), according to al-Khalīl, and that it is subject to metathesis, hence *ṭas'*, or assimilation, hence *ṭa'z*.[57] What *al-'Ayn* has is as follows: "*al-ṭasi': al-rajul alladhī lā ghīra lahu*" (a man with no sense of honor).[58] In the same entry, al-Khalīl mentions *ṭazi'a* as a variant of *ṭasi'a*, and in the entry *ṭ-z-'* he mentions *ṭazi'* with the same meaning as *ṭasi'*.[59] The distortion in Ibn Durayd's mind is apparent: the meaning he assigns to the word is remotely related to what al-Khalīl mentions --- the common element in both being the relation between a man and a woman --- and the assimilated form for Ibn Durayd is *ṭa's*, while for al-Khalīl it is *ṭazi'* from *ṭasi'*. It is noteworthy also that the root *ṭ-'-s* is *muhmal* (unused) according to al-Khalīl.[60]

(j) He attributes to al-Khalīl that *mindīl* (handkerchief) is a *mif'īl* form derived from *nadilat yaduhu* [61] i.e., "his hand became greasy." Nothing of this sort is mentioned by al-Khalīl in the entry *n-*

d-l.[62]

(k) He also attributes to al-Khalīl that *mash'* is a Yamanī word for teasing cotton,[63] but this is not found in *al-'Ayn*, at least not under *m-sh-'*[64] which has other meanings there.

(l) He indicates that al-Khalīl did not mention *faka'*.[65] The root *f-k-'* is indeed *muhmal* (unused) in *al-'Ayn*.[66]

(m) He explains the entry *m-'-s*[67] while al-Khalīl says that it is *muhmal*.[68]

(n) He rejects as impermissible the use of *yarkuḍ* (to run) instead of *yurkaḍ* (to be made to run) in relation to a horse.[69] Al-Khalīl, however, confirms that *yarkuḍ* is a used form.[70]

The above instances reveal the following facts about the relationship between *al-'Ayn* and *al-Jamhara*:

(1) That some of Ibn Durayd's quotations from al-Khalīl are not exact, and their *riwāya* is somewhat distorted, as in (a), (b), and (i) above.

(2) That he exercises his independent judgment by criticizing some of al-Khalīl's explanations or by rejecting them and indicating his own ignorance of the true meaning, as in (c) and (d).

(3) That he attributes to Layth some of the errors in *al-'Ayn*, as in (e) and (f). In this, Ibn Durayd is in agreement with a large sector of ancient scholars who, by proposing that Layth concluded what al-Khalīl started in this book, find it easy to explain any weakness in *al-'Ayn* by blaming it on Layth, thus avoiding the embarrassment of attributing error to al-Khalīl himself.

For Ibn Durayd, there seems to be no doubt that *al-'Ayn* is the work of al-Khalīl, and the introduction of *al-Jamhara*[71] is very clear in that respect. Thus, his method of charging Layth with error is more a polite way of criticizing al-Khalīl himself than an attempt to cover up for him.

(4) That, in certain cases, he seems not to be aware of material

in *al-'Ayn*, as in (g) and (h).

(5) That some of the explanations he attributes to al-Khalīl are not found in *al-'Ayn*, as in (j) and (k). Since the possibility of these instances being references to some other book by al-Khalīl is almost non-existent, the only plausible explanation --- excluding error --- is that they were not preserved in extant manuscripts.

(6) That he presents material unavailable in *al-'Ayn* (m) and comments on usage permissible to al-Khalīl (n).

The question of *shawāhid* [72] provides yet another angle from which the relationship between the two works can be examined. It is clear that some of the *shawāhid* are common to both, and this is easy to explain since much of the linguistic and grammatical data occurs in the sources. What is strange, however, is that the common *shawāhid* are far fewer than the ones unique to either. A glance at the footnotes of the new edition of *al-Jamhara*, where reference to the *shawāhid* of *al-'Ayn* is standard, reveals that material in common is only a fraction of the individual material. For example, the number of *shawāhid* [73] in the section on the sound biliteral roots in *al-Jamhara*,[74] excluding any repeated *shāhid*, is 630, out of which only fifty-eight occur in *al-'Ayn*. Conversely, *al-'Ayn* contains a large number of *shawāhid* that do not occur in *al-Jamhara*, or indeed in any other source.[75] Ibn Durayd's disregard for many of al-Khalīl's *shawāhid* adversely affected their currency since Ibn Durayd was a major source for later authors who seem not to have directly benefitted from *al-'Ayn*.

Al-Jamhara's distinctness from *al-'Ayn* becomes evident once more. Ibn Durayd's reliance on certain works that appeared after al-Khalīl is further proof of this. These include *Majāz al-Qur'ān* by Abū 'Ubayda (d. A.H. 210/A.D. 825) and *al-Ḥamz* by Abū Zayd, both of which Ibn Durayd almost totally incorporated in his work. *Ma'ānī al-shi'r* by Ushnāndānī (d. A.H. 288/A.D. 900) --- which reached us through Ibn Durayd's *riwāya* --- is another example. It is no wonder, therefore, that Ibn al-Tayyānī (d. A.H. 436/A.D. 1044) composed a treatise, called *al-Mū'ab*, in which he included the material found in *al-Jamhara* but not in *al-'Ayn*.[76] In the light of this, it is hard to believe that *al-Jamhara* is a mere version of *al-'Ayn* or that Ibn Durayd is a mere transmitter of its material.

On the question of the internal arrangement of the material within each entry, any attempt at finding significant and clear-cut differences between the two works is bound to be futile, as neither author has an explicit method of arranging the elements of his entries. Naṣṣār tries to outline differences between the two authors concerning the internal arrangement of the entries, claiming that al-Khalīl is more consistent than Ibn Durayd in indicating the singular and plural forms of nouns, indicating past, present, and verbal noun forms for verbs, placing intransitive verbs before transitive ones, and showing the derivational links between forms.[77] This claim is impossible to substantiate and is no more than an impressionistic view that can be invalidated by a random comparison between a few entries.

Al-Khalīl, to whom Arabic lexicography is so heavily indebted, had mixed fortunes with his contemporaries as well as with the later authors. His lexicon was not transmitted by contemporaries, some of whom, we are told, like Mu'arrij al-Sadūsī (d. A.H. 195/A.D. 810), Naḍr ibn Shumayl (d. A.H. 203/A.D. 818), Naṣr ibn 'Alī (d. A.H. 250/A.D. 864), and Abū al-Ḥasan al-Akhfash (d. A.H. 215/A.D. 830) were not aware of it for a long time.[78] Not few of the early authors took the extreme line of denying al-Khalīl any credit for the work.[79]

On the other hand, his great achievements in lexicography, grammar, and prosody have caused some --- as was pointed out earlier --- not to ascribe any error in *al-'Ayn* to al-Khalīl himself but to transmitters and text corruption. Al-Khalīl's accomplishments, especially his setting of the principles for exhausting usage through roots, should not, however, deter researchers from seeing minor as well as major points of difference between him and later authors, especially Ibn Durayd, whose vast treatise represents a major milestone in Arabic lexicography and who is relatively close in time to al-Khalīl. The long-held view that *al-Jamhara* is a modified version of *al-ʿAyn*, it must be concluded, is more myth than reality.

Notes

1. Yāqūt, *Muʿjam-al-udabāʾ*, ed. A.F. Rifāʿī. (Cairo, 1936-1938), 18:138. Cf. Suyūṭī, *al-Muzhir fī ʿulūm al-lugha wa-anwāʿihā*, ed. M.A. Jād al-Mawlā et al. (Cairo n.d.), 1:94. It is interesting to note that Nifṭawayhi's lines have been expanded by an unknown poet quoted by Yāqūt (*Muʿjam al-udabāʾ*, 17:47) from the back cover of a copy of Azharī's *Tahdhīb al-lugha*. This new addition also alleges that Azharī's *Tahdhīb* and Kharazanjī's *Takmila* are two other plagiarized works taken from *al-ʿAyn!*

2. Especially because of the pun Ibn Durayd invents for the name Nifṭawayhi, whereby he wishes his adversary to be burnt by *nifṭ* and lamented by *wayhi (aḥraqahu-l-lāhu bi-nisf ismihi wa-ṣayyara l-bāqī ṣurākhan ʿalayhi)*.

3. Jawālīqī, *al-Muʿarrab min al-kalām al-aʿjamī* (Cairo, 1361), 288, n.1.

4. *al-Maʿājim al-lughawiyya fī ḍawʾ dirāsāt ʿilm al-lugha al-ḥadīth* (Beirut 1966), 27.

5. *al-Muzhir* 1:94

6. Ḥusayn Naṣṣār, *al-Muʿjam al-ʿarabī: nashʾatuhu wa-taṭawwuruhu* (Cairo 1956), esp. 428.

7. Cf. the long list compiled by G. ʿAbābina, *Makānat al-Khalīl ibn Aḥmad fī l-naḥw al-ʿarabī* (Amman 1984), 158-176. This list includes phonetic terms as well. Among the grammatical terms, we find *rafʿ*, *naṣb*, *jarr*, *ḍamm*, *fatḥ*, *kasr*, *ism*, *fiʿl*, *ḥarf*, *mubtadaʾ*, *khabar*, *iḍāfa*, *naʿt*, *ʿatf*, *badal*, *tawkīd*, *ḥāl*, *istithnāʾ*, *ẓarf*, *nidāʾ*, *tanwīn*, etc...

8. *Kitāb al-ʿayn*, ed. M. al-Makhzūmī and I. al-Samarrāʾī. (Baghdad, 1980-85), 1:48; 57.

9. Ibid. 1:48. Cf. 1:49 for his refinement of this stipulation, according to whether nouns or verbs are concerned.

10. Translation by John A. Haywood, *Arabic Lexicography: Its History and its Place in the General History of Lexicography* (Leiden, 1960), 46.

11. Ibid., 38-9.

12. Cf. the divisions of al-Khalīl with those of Ibn Durayd as detailed in the introduction of *al-Jamhara*, ed. by R. Baalbaki. (Beirut, 1987-88), 16-18.

13. To illustrate but one division, we note that the quadriliteral roots duplicated with a *hamza* -- such as *sʾsʾ*, *ṣʾṣʾ*, and *ṭʾṭʾ* -- are assembled in a special *bāb* of *al-Jamhara* (226-28), whereas al-Khalīl mentions *sʾsʾ* with the *lafīf* of *sīn*; i.e. with *syʾ*, *syy*, *swy*, *swʾ*, *sʾw*, *ʾws*, *ʾys*, *ās*, *wys*, *swy*, *ʾsy*, *ʾsw*, *syh*, *ʾss*, *wsws*, and *sws* (*al-ʿAyn* 7:325-27), *ṣʾṣʾ* with the *lafīf* of *ṣād* (7:175-76), and *ṭʾṭʾ* with the *lafīf* of *ṭāʾ* (7:470).

14. These roots appear in a separate index in Baalbaki's edition of *al-Jamhara*. See index 9, "*fihris al-judhūr ghayr al-wārida fī abwābihā*", 1663-89.

15. In addition to this, the root accidentally occurs in two other places (53; 875); i.e., not as an entry in its own right.

16. *al-Jamhara*, 128, 234, 809, 1069, 1195, 1247, 1256, 1267, 1290.

17. Ibid., 351, 1023, 1259, 1276, 1290, 1291, 1302, 1333, 1336.

18. For other instances of such recurrence, see index 8 of *al-Jamhara*, 1565-1661.

19. Note also the recurrence of *shawāhid* (poetry, proverbs, Quranic verses, etc.) in these sections, as shown in footnotes to the text, esp. those in the latter section i.e., 1016-85. See also the striking recurrence of material on 239-40 in another section, 883-4.

20. Ibn Jinni, *al-Khaṣāʾiṣ*, ed. M.A. Najjār (Cairo, 1952-56), 3:288. See also *al-Muzhir,* 1:93.

21. Ibid., 1135. Cf. 893, 1124, 1140, 1142.

22. It should be noted that the section on quinqueliteral roots exhibits a very high degree of confusion. Here are included, for example, triconsonantal words of the form *fāʿūl* (e.g., *nāmūs*; 1205-7), quadriconsonantal words of the form *fuʿālil* (e.g., *qunādil*; 1208-13), and words ending with the feminine marker (e.g., *khilafnā* and *ʿiraḍnā*; 1223).

23. *Arabic lexicography,* 53.

24. *al-Muʿjam al-ʿarabī,* 427.

25. "The beginnings of Arabic lexicography till the time of Jauhari, with special reference to the work of Ibn Duraid." *JRAS*, Cent. Supp. (1924), 254ff.

26. *al-Jāsūs ʻalā l-qāmūs* (Constantinople, 1299), 521.

27. See *supra*, p. 48, section (3), paragraph 2.

28. See the titles of these chapters (1247-1337) in the general index, 1778-80.

29. *Arabic Lexicography,* 53.

30. See 1162-1247.

31. Ibn Sidah, *al-Mukhaṣṣaṣ*, (Bulaq 1316-21), 1:10.

32. *al-ʻAyn* 1:52.

33. Ibid., 1:53.

34. See the index, 1521.

35. Ibid., 1743.

36. *al-Jamhara*, 696.

37. *al-ʻAyn*, 1:244.

38. *al-Jamhara*, 841.

39. Ibid., 1270.

40. *al-ʻAyn*, 1:333.

41. The possibility of *samīn* having the meaning of *masmūn* (i.e., as *faʻīl* and *mafʻūl* can be synonyms) is negated by the text itself where another view given is that *ʻalīs* is neither *samīn* nor *mahzūl*.

42. Cf. my introduction to *al-Jamhara*, 23.

43. *al-Jamhara*, 645.

44. *al-ʻAyn*, 321.

45. *al-Jamhara*, 887.

46. *al-ʻAyn*, 1:315.

47. *al-Jamhara,* 651.

48. *al-ʻAyn, sadafa,* 7:230; *shadafa,* 6:244.

49. *al-Jamhara,* 260.

50. *al-ʻAyn,* 4:402.

51. Ibid., 2:112.

52. *Lisān al-ʻarab (bʻth)*: Cf. Yāqūt al-Ḥamawī, *Muʻjam al-buldān*, (Beirut, 1955-57), 1:451 *(buʻāth)*.

53. *al-Jamhara,* 936.

54. *al-ʻAyn*, 1:176.

55. *al-Jamhara*, 365.

56. *al-ʻAyn,* 1:208.

57. *al-Jamhara,* 834.

58. *al-ʻAyn,* 1:321, where *ṭasiʻ* is unvocalized. Our vocalization is based upon the form *ṭazi'* which occurs in 1:351.

59. Ibid., 1:351.

60. Ibid., 1:319.

61. *al-Jamhara*, 682.

62. *al-'Ayn,* 8:41.

63. *al-Jamhara,* 870.

64. 1:267.

65. *al-Jamhara,* 937.

66. 1:205.

67. *al-Jamhara,* 843.

68. *al-'Ayn,* 1:346.

69. *al-Jamhara*, 750.

70. *al-'Ayn,* 5:301.

71. Esp. 40.

72. Used here exclusively for poetic *shawāhid.*

73. Considering each line of poetry and each hemistich of *rajaz* as one *shāhid.*

74. 53-172.

75. Cf. the footnotes of *al-'Ayn*, where a large number of *shawāhid* seem to be unique to this lexicon as no later source has preserved them according to the editors. See, however, some notes on the *takhrīj* of the editors in R. Baalbaki's review of *Kitāb al-'Ayn*, in *al-Abḥāth*, 34 (1986), 87-96, esp. 89f

76. 'Alī ibn Yūsuf al-Qifṭī, *Inbāh al-ruwāt 'alā anbāh al-nuḥāt,* ed. M.A. Ibrāhīm (Cairo, 1950-73), 1:295. Cf. *al-Muzhir* 1:88.

77. *al-Mu'jam al-'arabī,* 427.

78. *al-Muzhir,* 1:84.

79. Especially al-Azharī who, in *Tahdhīb al-lugha* (Cairo, 1964), 1:28, claims that the lexicon is by al-Layth who attributed it to al-Khalīl to ensure its circulation.

Al-Khalīl Ibn Aḥmad and Music

Eckhard Neubauer

The eminent role played by al-Khalīl ibn Aḥmad al-Farāhīdī (d.ca. A.H. 175/A.D. 791) in early philology has often been emphasized, and sometimes even overemphasized, as being that of a "founder" who had "invented" Arabic lexicography, grammar, and prosody.[1] This opinion was due to the precipitous development of these disciplines effected by al-Khalīl between the generation of his teachers, such as ʿĪsā ibn ʿUmar al-Thaqafī (d. A.H. 149/A.D. 766), Abū ʿAmr ibn al-ʿAlāʾ (d.ca. A.H. 154/A.D. 771) and that of his pupils, to name but the celebrated Sībawayh (d.ca. A.H. 180/A.D. 796) and ʿAbd al-Malik ibn Qurayb al-Aṣmaʿī (d. A.H. 213/A.D. 828). With extraordinary effectiveness al-Khalīl carried on, systematically enlarged the work done by his predecessors, and assimilated more than one stimulating idea arising in the internationally minded society of his hometown, Basra.

The numerous essential quotations referring to al-Khalīl in Sībawayh's *Kitāb* testify to his outstanding erudition in grammar.[2] His great lexicon, the *Kitāb al-ʿayn*, although not finished by himself, is rightly considered a landmark of early perfection in Arabic lexicography.[3] In its arrangement, which seems to display Indian influence, it reveals the stimulation of the multicultural Basran milieu.[4] Similarly, an initial idea of depicting prosodic meters by symbols may have been suggested by the Indian model, as conjectured by some early Arab or Persian authorities,[5] which in no way diminishes al-Khalīl's lasting celebrity resulting from his depiction and classification of *ʿarūḍ*.[6] Unlike these well-known accomplishments in lexicography, grammar, and prosody, al-Khalīl's less spectacular interest in other fields, such as theology, falconry,[7] or music, is still rather unknown. He was, after all, one of the early writers on music theory in Islam. A *Kitāb al-nagham* on the "notes," i.e., the tonal system underlying the melodic modes, and a *Kitāb al-īqāʿ* on musical meter and rhythm are attributed to him in the *Fihrist* of Ibn al-Nadīm (d. A.H. 380/A.D. 990).[8]

As no manuscript nor quotations from al-Khalīl's work on music seems to have survived, I propose here to develop an approximate idea about his contribution to the history of Arabic music theory.[9] This will be done by evaluating relevant source material, not only with regard to al-Khalīl himself, but also with regard to his predecessor, Yūnus al-Kātib (d.ca. A.H. 147/A.D. 765) and to his successor, Isḥāq ibn Ibrāhīm al-Mawṣilī (d. A.H. 235/A.D. 850), who was a student of al-Khalīl's pupil, al-Aṣmaʿī.

An early estimation of al-Khalīl's position in the history of music compared to that of Isḥāq al-Mawṣilī is to be found in the introduction to a book on the "Ranks of Musicians" (*Ṭabaqāt al-mughannīn*), which was written in A.H. 215/A.D. 830 and is attributed to al-Jāḥiẓ (d. A.H. 255/A.D. 869) in the only copy that has survived.[10] There it states that "the Arabs had no knowledge of the foundations (*ʿilal*) [of music], its constitutional [or metrical] parts (*asbāb*), metrical substance [compared to prosody] (*wazn*) and rules of 'flection' (*taṣārīf*). Their knowledge of music was casual (*ʿalā l-hājis*) and based on what they had learned from the Persians and

Indians, until al-Khalīl set up his theory about poetry and its meters (*naẓara fī l-shiʿr wa-waznihi*).... After he had successfully finished (*aḥkama*) and achieved (*balagha*) what he could achieve therein, he set about explaining the notes and melodies (*akhadha fī tafsīr al-nagham wa-l-luḥūn*). He attained something in this area (*istadraka minhu shayʾan*), and gave a depiction (*rasm*) of it that could be taken as example by those who succeeded him (*iḥtadhā ʿalayhi man khalafahu*) and from which those who were devoted to [the subject] could draw [their knowledge] (*istamaddahu man ʿuniya bihi*). The first to do so was Isḥāq ibn Ibrāhīm al-Mawṣilī. He followed his direction, combining [in his person] competences which were wanting in his predecessor, al-Khalīl ibn Aḥmad. Among them was his professional knowledge of music (*maʿrifatuhu bi-l-ghināʾ*), his frequent listening to it (*kathrat istimāʿihi iyyāhu*), and his capability of distinguishing between good and bad, correct and incorrect music (*ʿilmuhu bi-ḥasanihi min qabīḥihi wa-ṣaḥīḥihi min saqīmihi*). There was furthermore his excellent ability in lute playing and keeping the meter, and his knowledge of [the melodies...and their[11]] prosodic meters (*ḥidhquhu bi-l-ḍarb wa-l-īqāʿ wa-ʿilmuhu bi-* [*l-luḥūn...wa-*] *waznihā*). He wrote prodigious books (*kutub muʿjiba*) about it, finding easy what was hard (*mustaṣʿib*) for others.[12]

This noble appreciation of al-Khalīl's merits in the field of music theory conveys, nevertheless, the impression that his achievements were rather modest compared to the splendid contributions made later by Isḥāq al-Mawṣilī. An attitude of lukewarm approval of al-Khalīl's writings on music prevails then in most of the remaining sources, except for those articulating criticism or sheer disapproval. In contradiction to the statement found in the *Ṭabaqāt al-mughannīn*, the Muʿtazilite al-Jāḥiẓ voiced in his *Kitāb al-ḥayawān* a very harsh critique reminiscent of a general verdict uttered against al-Khalīl by the Muʿtazilite Ibrāhīm ibn Sayyār al-Naẓẓām (d. A.H. 231/A.D. 845), much admired by al-Jāḥiẓ. Al-Naẓẓām had accused al-Khalīl of megalomania and mental confusion (*junūn; ikhtilāṭ al-ʿaql*).[13] Along the same lines, al-Jāḥiẓ states that "al-Khalīl ibn Aḥmad, after successfully treating grammar (*naḥw*) and prosody (*ʿarūḍ*), thought he could do the same with theology (*kalām*) and the composition of melodies (*taʾlīf al-luḥūn*). He wrote two books on these subjects which show nothing but mental illness (*al-mirra al-muḥtariqa*: burned bile)."[14] In an even cruder form, al-Jāḥiẓ's critique was transmitted by al-Marzubānī (d. A.H. 384/A.D. 944).[15] But also Ḥamza al-Iṣfahānī (d. before A.H. 360/A.D. 970) expressed himself with reservation when saying: "In the science of music and musical metrics (*ʿilm al-ghināʾ wa-l-īqāʿ*) [al-Khalīl] composed a book which he entitled 'Constituents of Songs' (*Tarākīb al-aṣwāt*), although he never had touched a chord (*watar*) nor a wand (*qaḍīb*) and seldom watched musicians (*lā kathurat mushāhadatuhu li-l-mughannīn*)."[16] And Abū ʿUbayd al-Bakrī (d. A.H. 487/A.D. 1094) echoed that "al-Khalīl composed a book on melodies and the 'constituents of songs' without ever having touched a string or having had intercourse with musicians."[17]

The last argument is not appropriate, and, on the whole, one should not overestimate such general attacks. Hardly any of the men of letters or philologists who expressed their views on al-Khalīl and music, or transmitted the opinion of others, had ever seen al-Khalīl's work on this subject or were capable to judge it. An exception was Isḥāq al-Mawṣilī, who explicitly praised his predecessor. We are told by Abū Bakr al-Zubaydī (d. A.H. 379/A.D. 989) the author of the well-known abridgement of al-Khalīl's *Kitāb al-ʿayn*, that Isḥāq, after completing his "Book on the Tonal and the Metrical Systems" (*Kitāb al-nagham wa-l-īqāʿ*), showed it to his princely colleague and rival,

Ibrāhīm ibn al-Mahdī (d. A.H. 224/A.D. 839) who applauded: "Bravo (*aḥsanta*), Abū Muḥammad, you did a very good job (*kathīran mā tuḥsinu*)." Whereupon Isḥāq replied: "Not I, it was al-Khalīl who did so well (*bal aḥsana l-Khalīl*), since he paved the way to successful accomplishment (*li-annahu ja'ala l-sabīl ilā l-iḥsān*)."[18] It is, however, possible that Isḥāq had intended not so much al-Khalīl's musical but his prosodic work, corresponding thus to the aforementioned passage from the *Ṭabaqāt al-mughannīn*, in which the book on *'arūḍ* was seen as an initial step towards music theory.

In the same text al-Khalīl is introduced as the first to have written on music theory in Islam. This is not correct and testifies to a lack of historical knowledge on the part of the author of the *Ṭabaqāt al-mughannīn*. It is true that al-Khalīl was one of the early authors in this area, but he was not the first. He was preceded at least by Yūnus al-Kātib, a scribe of Iranian origin who lived in Medina, visited the Umayyad court at Damascus, and died ca. A.H. 147/A.D. 765, maybe in Baghdad.[19] According to Ibn al-Nadīm, Yūnus had already written a *Kitāb al-nagham*,[20] as al-Khalīl did later. Knowledge of early Arabic music literature is very limited; there are no traces of this book, and we are ignorant of any other work Yūnus (or anybody else in his generation) may have written on music theory. Aside from the *Kitāb al-nagham*, Ibn al-Nadīm knew only of Yūnus's "Book on the Singing-Girls" (*Kitāb al-qiyān*) and the collection of his own compositions, i.e., song texts called *Kitāb al-mujarrad li-Yūnus*.[21] As far as Yūnus's famous song book (*Kitāb fī l-aghānī*,[22] otherwise called *Dīwān Yūnus*)[23] is concerned, there is no mention of it in Ibn al-Nadīm's *Fihrist*, although it became the starting point and the primary source of a new literary genre culminating two centuries later in the *Kitāb al-aghānī al-kabīr* by Abū al-Faraj al-Iṣfahānī (d.A.H. 356/A.D. 967).

When we turn to al-Khalīl's titles on music, the sources display a similar uncertainty. Ibn al-Nadīm lists a *Kitāb al-nagham* and a *Kitāb al-īqā'*.[24] This information was repeated by Yāqūt al-Ḥamawī (d. A.H. 626/A.D. 1229),[25] in contrast to other authors of biographical dictionaries and handbooks who list either the first or the second title, but never both.[26] As a rule, when al-Khalīl's work on music is mentioned, only one title or book is intended. Ḥamza al-Iṣfahānī (d. before A.H. 360/A.D 970) says that al-Khalīl composed a book on music (*'ilm al-ghinā'*) and musical metrics (*īqā'*) in which he treated the "constituents of songs" (*tarākīb al-aṣwāt*).[27]

Similarly, Abū 'Ubayd al-Bakrī (d. A.H. 487/A.D. 1094) calls it a book on melodies and, again, the "constituents of songs" (*alḥān wa-tarākīb al-aṣwāt*).[28] According to the *Ṭabaqāt al-mughannīn,* it was a book explaining notes and melodies (*fī tafsīr al-nagham wa-l-luḥūn*).[29] In al-Jāḥiẓ's *Kitāb al-ḥayawān,* it was called a book on the composition of melodies (*ta'līf al-luḥūn*).[30] Based on the authority of al-Jāḥiẓ, Abū al-Maḥāsin al-Tanūkhī (d. A.H. 442/A.D. 1050) ascribed to al-Khalīl a book on melodies (*Kitāb fī l-alḥān*),[31] whereas both Ibn al-Mu'tazz (d. A.H. 296/A.D. 908)[32] and al-Marzubānī (d. A.H. 384/A.D. 994)[33] knew of a "well-known book" by al-Khalīl on melodies and notes (*fī l-alḥān wa-l-nagham*).

The information given in these sources is of limited value and does not allow any serious conclusion concerning al-Khalīl's actual opus. Moreover, the most unusual title, *Kitāb tarākīb al-aṣwāt*, introduced by Ḥamza al-Iṣfahānī, neither corresponds to any customary music title in early Islam nor does it make sense with respect to the musical terminology of the time --- it may have been a philologist's transpostion of the musical expression "composition of melodies" (*ta'līf al-alḥān*). For lack of sound evidence, the titles

Kitāb al-nagham and *Kitāb al-īqā'* testified to by Ibn al-Nadīm are, therefore, to be considered the closest approximation to what al-Khalīl may have written. If it really was a single book, as most of the sources suggest, it may have borne the title, *Kitāb al-nagham wa-l-īqā',* like Isḥāq al-Mawṣilī's major work on music theory.

As far as the topic of *nagham* is concerned, we can suppose that al-Khalīl was not the man to add anything of importance to the contemporary discussion. It would have required a sound knowledge of the fingerboard of the lute and of the structure of the basic octave represented on the frets, such as could scarcely be expected of a layman. For a description of the "notes" he thus must have depended on more professional sources and authorities, such as Yūnus al-Kātib.

Nothing having survived from either Yūnus's or al-Khalīl's texts, we have to rely on further, i.e., later sources if we want to secure some notion of the early *nagham* system. Its oldest known depiction goes back to Isḥāq al-Mawṣilī. Quotations from one of his lost books convey a vivid impression of the level reached in this field two generations after al-Khalīl. The passages in question are contained in the earliest extant *Kitāb al-nagham*, written by Yaḥyā ibn 'Alī ibn Yaḥyā al-Munajjim (d. A.H. 300/A.D. 913).[34] Ibn al-Munajjim was directly related to the Mawṣilian school tradition and acted as an intermediary between Isḥāq al-Mawṣilī and Abū l-Faraj al-Iṣfahānī in musical and literary respects. His father, 'Alī ibn Yaḥyā al-Munajjim (d. A.H. 275/A.D. 888), a personal friend of Isḥāq, had written a biographical *Kitāb akhbār Isḥāq ibn Ibrāhīm al-Mawṣilī.*[35] It was transmitted by Yaḥyā to Abū l-Faraj who extensively used it for Isḥāq's biography in the *Kitāb al-aghānī.*[36] Ibn al-Munajjim's *Kitāb al-nagham* was composed in order to discuss the number of "notes" common to the music theory of the time, and to explain Isḥāq's new terminology for classifying the traditional scales underlying the modes.

Disregarding the questions raised by Isḥāq al-Mawsilī's classification, we can abstract from Ibn al-Munajjim's text the following basic data concerning the concept of *nagham*. This "group of notes" (*nagham*, fem. coll.) forms a Pythagorean scale. It is limited, for theoretical purposes, to the range of a major seventh, whereby the repetition of the basic note in the higher octave is avoided. The scale includes a major and a minor third, a minor and a major sixth, and a minor seventh. The single notes (*naghamāt*, sing. *naghma*) are named according to their position on the fingerboard of the lute and are numbered one to ten by the use of the letters of the alphabet in their numerical value:

1.(*alif*): Second highest string, open position (*muṭlaq al-mathnā*). This note is considered the basic note of the system; it is used in tuning (like the a' of our violins), and therefore called the "pillar" (*ʿimād*).

2. (*bāʾ*): First finger (*sabbāba*) on the *mathnā* string a major second above the open string.

3. (*jīm*): Second finger (*wusṭā*) on the same string, a minor third.

4. [*dāl*: Omitted in the MSS]: Third finger (*binṣir*) on the same string, a major third.

5. (*hāʾ*): Fourth finger (*khinṣir*) on the same string, identical with the note of the highest open string (*zīr*), a perfect fourth.

6. (*wāw*): First finger on the *zīr* string, a perfect fifth.

7. (*zāy*): Second finger on the same string, a minor sixth.

8. (*ḥāʾ*): Third finger on the same string, a major sixth.

9. (*ṭāʾ*): Fourth finger on the same string, a minor seventh.

10. (*yāʾ*): First finger on the *binṣir* position, the string being stopped with the third finger; a major seventh.

[11. (*yāʾ-alif*): Fourth finger in the same position: the higher octave of the "pillar." This note, although used in practice, was excluded from the theoretical system, as were the notes of the lower octave on the lower two strings.]

This was the system of *nagham* as described in the third century A.H. (ninth century A.D.) by Ibn al-Munajjim.[37] There would be no reason to assume that a century earlier al-Khalīl would have been able to give more information about it, except that he had perhaps also mentioned the corresponding eight notes of the lower two strings of the lute. Apart from this, his contribution can be seen as having been limited to an even less detailed exposition of the above ten basic notes of the *nagham* system (*al-naghamāt al-ʿashr*).[38]

It is indeed difficult to think about anything else al-Khalīl's *Kitāb al-nagham* could have contained. The problem of the correct scope of the system of notes and their number, controversially discussed by the theorists of Arab music (*aṣḥāb al-ghināʾ al-ʿarabiyy*) and the advocates of Greek and Byzantine music theory (*aṣḥāb al-mūsīqī*), and first mentioned by Ibn al-Munajjim,[39] was not yet a subject to concern al-Khalīl ibn Aḥmad. More complicated topics such as the classification of scales or the question of chromaticism were also left to later generations and are connected first and foremost to the name of Isḥāq al-Mawṣilī. It was Isḥāq who developed the concept of the "courses" (*majārī*, sing. *majrā*) for defining scales (and modes) according to their mutually exclusive use of either the third or the fourth note of the above list (*fī majrā al-wusṭā* or *fī majrā al-binṣir*, as attested in the *Kitāb al-aghānī*). His text explaining this procedure was also transmitted by Ibn al-Munajjim in his *Kitāb al-nagham*.[40] As a consequence of Isḥāq's classification of the scales, the question arose of how to explain notes that were alien to the basic scale or mode of a song. This problem was treated by Isḥāq in a book called *Kitāb al-nagham wa- ʿilalihā*,[41] by Ibn al-Munajjim at the end of his *Kitāb al-nagham*,[42] and by Abū al-Faraj al-Iṣfahānī in a *Risāla fī ʿilal al-nagham*.[43] All these topics belonged to the further evolution of the *nagham* theory after al-Khalīl's time.

We can likewise, for several reasons, dismiss the possibility that in al-Khalīl's *nagham* book the concept of "mode" was discussed. To begin with, the word *nagham* (pl. *anghām*) received its connotation of "mode" at a distinctly later date. The first known book on *maʿrifat al-anghām* which testifies to this development, was written in the year A.H. 729/A.D. 1329.[44]

Moreover, it seems that in al-Khalīl's time not just one but several denonimations of modes were known. One was derived from the Syro-Byzantine system of the eight modes, called *oktōēchos*.[45] This term was translated into Arabic as *al-luḥūn al-thamāniya*. Accordingly, and in correspondance to the Byzantine custom, the modes were called *al-laḥn al-awwāl* (*ēchos prōtos*), *al-laḥn al-thānī* (*ēchos deuteros*), and so forth. They were used prior to the time of Ibrāhīm al-Mawṣilī, as Ibn al-Ṭaḥḥān (d. after A.H. 449/A.D. 1057) relates: At that time "one knew the *ṭarīqa* [the 'way' of a melody, see below] by its *laḥn* [= mode], whereas in our days, one knows the *laḥn* [= melody] by its *ṭarīqa*." [46] It is a telling example of the close relationship between, and interchange of, musical styles in Umayyad

Syria and reminds us of the fact that Yūnus al-Kātib was a younger contemporary of John of Damascus (d.ca. A.D. 750), the legendary "inventor" of the *oktōēchos*. A pseudo-Ptolemaic *Kitāb al-luḥūn al-thamāniya*, also called *Kitāb al-mūsīqī*, was mentioned by as early a writer as Ibn al-Kalbī (d.ca. A.H. 204/A.D. 819), presumably in his lost book on the "Beginnings of the Arabian Music and the Lutes" (*Kitāb ibtidā' al-ghinā' wa-l-'īdān*).[47]

In distinction to this early testimony to the *oktōēchos* - *laḥn* system of the eight modes, another system, which was also derived from the Graecophone culture, was mentioned in Arabic at a later date. Ya'qūb ibn Isḥāq al-Kindī (d. after A.H. 256/A.D. 870) briefly describes a system of seven modes called *ṭanīnāt* (sing. *ṭanīn*, the Greek *tónoi*, sing. *tónos*), a term which he equates with *laḥn/luḥūn*.[48] Although, on the one hand, we do not know whether or not this system was of relevance for the musical scene in al-Khalīl's lifetime, we cannot, on the other hand, exclude the notion that it was known among Arabic-speaking musicians prior to al-Kindī. According to the "philosopher of the Arabs," this system of seven modes, to which he had devoted a whole book called *Kitāb al-a'ẓam fī ta'līf al-luḥūn*,[49] was the most correct modal system compared to five others that he mentions by the number of their modes (*luḥūn*), namely, three, four, six, thirteen, and fifteen.[50]

The modal systems of Syria, Iran, and Ḥijāz must have resembled each other to such extent in late antiquity and early Islam that any kind of musical and terminological transculturation was possible.[51] The singer Ibn Misjaḥ (d.c.a. A.H. 90/710) was one of those who adapted melodies of the Byzantines (*alḥān al-rūm*), of the Persians (*barbaṭiyya*), and of the Syrians (*usṭūkhūsiyya*, i.e., belonging to the *oktōēchos*) to the musical taste of the Arabs.[52] As for the Persians, one of the common names for "mode" in al-Khalīl's time was an Iranian derivate. It occurs in a short description of Sassanian art and court music given by Ibn Khurradādhbih (d. A.H. 300/A.D. 913), where he says that "the music of the Persians was played on lutes (*ʻīdān*) and harps (*ṣunūj*). These instruments were proper to them as was the [knowledge of the] 'notes' (*nagham*) and the meters (*īqāʻāt*) with their principal notes (*maqāṭiʻ*, '*finales*'), and the modes (*ṭurūq*)".[53] The "Royal Modes" (*al-ṭurūq al-mulūkiyya*), intended in this text, were of the number of seven,[54] whereas the "melodies of the [Persian] *barbaṭ*-players" (*al-alḥān al-barbaṭiyya*) known to Ibn Misjaḥ may have been related to the "modes of [the Sassanian singer] Bārbad" which are reported to have been thirty.[55] The Arabic term *ṭarīqa* (pl. *ṭarāʼiq*) occurring in Ibn Khurradādhbih's text in the unusual plural form *ṭurūq* (in analogy to *luḥūn*?), denotes the "way" a melody develops. It was an equivalent to the Persian term *rāh*.[56]

The notion of *ṭarīqa*, as handed down in post-Khalīlian sources, implied an emphasis on the metrical component (*īqāʻ*) of the melody.[57] The melodic component (*laḥn*) could even be withheld, as exemplified in the song captions given by Ibn Khurradādhbih[58] or in Abū Bakr al-Ṣūlī's (d. A.H. 335/A.D. 964) *Kitāb al-awrāq*. Here we read of songs *fī ṭarīqat al-thaqīl al-awwal*,[59] *fī ṭarīqat khafīf al-thaqīl*,[60] *fī ṭarīqat al-ramal*,[61] *fī ṭarīqat al-ramal al-thānī*,[62] and the like. It must have been very common to describe a melody in this way by, its meter instead of by its melodic mode.[63]

In a more elaborate system of *ṭarīqa*, described in Syria by al-Ḥasan ibn Aḥmad ibn ʻAlī al-Kātib (early fifth century A.H./eleventh century A.D.) and in Egypt by Ibn al-Ṭaḥḥān (d. after A.H. 449/A.D. 1057), the four modes called *al-muṭlaq*, *al-mazmūm*, *al-maḥmūl*, and *al-maḥṣūr* (with a subgroup embracing *al-mujannab*, *al-munsariḥ*, *al-wusṭā*, and *al-mumakhkhir*) were regarded as subdivisions (*anwāʻ*) of the eight *īqāʻ* metres *al-thaqīl al-awwal*, *al-thaqīl al-thānī*, etc., (see below), whereby the central and/or final note of *al-muṭlaq* was note number 1 in the above list, that of *al-mazmūm* number 2, of *al-maḥmūl* number 3, and of *al-maḥṣūr* number 4.[64] A *ṭarīqat al-hazaj al-muṭlaq* [65] in this terminology was a melody in the *hazaj* meter and the mode called *al-muṭlaq*. It may have corresponded to a *ṭarīqat al-hazaj bi-l-wusṭā*,[66] a melody in the *hazaj* meter and the mode *al-muṭlaq fī majrā al-wusṭā*, in Isḥāq al-Mawṣilī's terminology.

In any case, the mode names in al-Khalīl's time must have differed from those familiar to us from the *Kitāb al-aghānī al-kabīr*, since Abū al-Faraj had adopted the *majrā* terminology of Isḥāq al-Mawṣilī (... *fī majrā al-wusṭā*, or ... *fī majrā al-binṣir*),[67] and thereby had suppressed differing terms. There is a high degree of probability that the mode names *al-muṭlaq*, *al-mazmūm* and the like, which survived the Mawṣilian terms in Iraq and Syria (al-Ḥasan ibn Aḥmad al-Kātib),[68] and were common in Egypt (Ibn al-Ṭaḥḥān) and in Muslim Spain,[69] were older than those attributed to Isḥāq al-Mawṣilī.

It is of interest in this connection that, according to Ibn Khurradādhbih, Yūnus al-Kātib had omitted the *ṭarīqa* indications (*ajnās*, sing. *jins*) in his famous song book.[70] This may have resulted from the differing terminologies of his sources. Instead of preferring one of them to the other and unifying his text accordingly, as Abū al-Faraj did two centuries later, Yūnus may have left out the terms altogether in order not to confuse his readers. The *ṭarīqa* names were added later by redactors and annotators of his book (in the respective terminology of their time and region) and eventually changed again when being incorporated into the *Kitāb al-aghānī*, unless they already corresponded to Isḥāq's system.[71] At any rate, al-Khalīl was certainly not the person to unify the modal terminology of his time. This work was commenced during the next generation by authorities such as Ibn Jāmi' (d. prior to A.H. 188/A.D. 804) and his rival Ibrāhīm al-

Mawṣilī, and it was continued by Isḥāq al-Mawṣilī.

Our considerations about al-Khalīl's lost *Kitāb al-nagham* can be concluded with the result that modes and modal structures were not, as far as we see now, a subject of early *nagham* literature. They were regarded as different theoretical disciplines and hence were discussed, if at all, under the headings of "modes" (*luḥūn*), "melodies" (*alḥān*; *luḥūn*) or "composition" (*ta'līf*; *ta'līf al-nagham*; *ta'līf al-luḥūn*; *ta'līf al-alḥān*).[72]

Had al-Khalīl really treated the topic of *ta'līf al-luḥūn* or *ta'līf al-alḥān* as stated by al-Jāḥiẓ and others, he would have done it independently of the topic of *nagham*. One of the above mode systems, presumably in the *ṭarīqa* form, would then have been his subject. But since that system was based on meter (*īqā'*), any discussion of the *ṭarīqa* would have presupposed a treatment of the meters.

One could expect that al-Khalīl played a more traceable role in the literature on *īqā'* than in that of *nagham*. After all, his *Kitāb al-īqā'* is the earliest title of its kind known in the sources, and musical metrics are traditionally related to al-Khalīl's special field of prosodic metrics. The statement "*īqā'* has the same place (*manzila*) in music as *'arūḍ* in poetry" was attributed to Isḥāq al-Mawṣilī.[73] There was another remark to the effect that al-Khalīl's knowledge of music had "created" for him the science of *'arūḍ* (*kānat ma'rifatuhu bi-l-īqā' huwa lladhī aḥdatha lahu 'ilm al-'arūḍ*).[74] It seems that this may originate from and belong to the realm of legendary traditions connecting al-Khalīl with Pythagoras[75] and is, therefore, open to question.

Nothing has survived of al-Khalīl's contribution to the *īqā'* theory, and his name is not mentioned in any extant early or later texts on the subject. In addition, our knowledge about the details of *īqā'* in theory and practice prior to al-Khalīl and during his lifetime is still sparse.

Nevertheless, one can start out from the notion that musical meters were as common to composers and singers in early Islam as prosodic meters were to the poets and their *ruwāt*.[76] In a basic text on the essentials of music making attributed to the singer Ibn Surayj (d. A.D. 96/A.D. 714), and praised by the famous Maʿbad (d.ca. A.H. 125/A.D. 743) as being comparable to a relevation (*qurʾān*) in the field of music, not only the prosodic meters (*awzān*) of the song texts, but also the "species" of musical meters (*ajnās al-īqāʿ*) are mentioned.[77] Ibn Surayj himself was known as a specialist for songs in one of these *ajnās* called *ramal*.[78] The number of the early "species" mentioned in later sources varies between six and eight. [79]

According to Ibn Khurradādhbih, Isḥāq al-Mawṣilī claimed that his father, Ibrāhīm al-Mawṣilī had "explained (*awḍaḥa*) the *īqāʿ* and given the names (*laqqaba*) to its eight species (*ajnās*): *al-thaqīl al-awwal*, *al-khafīf al-awwal*, *al-thaqīl al-thānī*, *al-khafīf al-thānī* alias *al-mākhūrī*, *al-ramal* (*al-awwal*), *khafīf al-ramal*, *hazaj*, and *khafīf al-hazaj*."[79] As with al-Khalīl ibn Aḥmad's "inventing" the *ʿarūḍ*, this assertion is not to be taken too literally. Ibrāhīm al-Mawṣilī was of course not the first to give names to the *īqāʿ* meters. He was involved in the process of defining, naming, and classifying them, and may have been the first to set up this special system which later on was described by his son Isḥāq. It is revealing that in books on music not the name of al-Khalīl ibn Aḥmad but rather that of Ibrāhīm al-Mawṣilī is connected with the development of *īqāʿ* prior to Isḥāq's generation. Even single meters are reported to have been introduced or named by Ibrāhīm, such as *al-mākhūrī* [80] or the two meters of *al-ramal* and *al-thaqīl al-awwal*.[81] Even during Isḥāq's time, the canon of the eight meters was not yet commonly accepted. Isḥāq and his rival, Ibrāhīm ibn al-Mahdī, held different opinions about the denomination of the two groups of *al-thaqīl/al-khafīf al-awwal* and *al-thaqīl/al-khafīf al-thānī*.[82] Apart from this, in musical practice several varieties of the eight Mawṣilian meters were in use, such as *ramal qadīm*,[83] *ramal muḥdath*,[84] *ramal ṭunbūrī*,[85] or *hazaj ṭunbūrī*,[86] which are not mentioned in the extant treatises on *īqāʿ*. The *Kitāb al-ʿayn* is of no help in the questions related to *īqāʿ* names since it does not contain any *īqāʿ* terminology. *Ramal*[87] and *hazaj*[88], for example, are listed solely as prosodic meters.

If al-Khalīl's lost *Kitāb al-īqāʿ* indeed contained the description of individual *īqāʿ* "species," their number ought to have been six to eight, as mentioned before, including *ramal* and *hazaj* as well as *thaqīl* and *khafīf* forms. It can be assumed that al-Khalīl was aware of the fundamental relationship between *ʿarūḍ* and *īqāʿ*, noticeable already by the overlap of their general terminologies. Since these were partly pre-Khalīlian, it is difficult to assess al-Khalīl's contribution to the *īqāʿ* theory in this respect. But if one accepts that al-Khalīl was the first to use *faʿala* forms and the symbols o and | for depicting the *ʿarūḍ* meters, one can anticipate that he tried to adopt the same means for depicting the "species" of *īqāʿ*. This was perhaps intended by the term *"rasm"* in the passage about al-Khalīl's work on music, quoted above from the *Ṭabaqāt al-mughannīn*.

Is there any evidence for a direct adoption of these *ʿarūḍ* patterns and symbols in early *īqāʿ* literature? The earliest extant definitions of *īqāʿ* meters go back to Isḥāq al-Mawṣilī and to Yaʿqūb ibn Isḥāq al-Kindī, the former being quoted by Abū Naṣr al-Fārābī (d. A.H. 339/A.D. 950). In Isḥāq's text on *īqāʿ* from his *Kitāb fī taʾlīf al-nagham*, preserved in al-Fārābī's *Kitāb iḥṣāʾ al-īqāʿāt*,[89] no connection at all to *'arūḍ* and its terminology is recognizable. On the other hand, we find an essential hint in this direction in the *Kitāb al-muṣawwitāt al-watariyya* (*Book of the Chordophones*) by al-Kindī.[90]

Speaking about the number eight and its relation to music, al-Kindī deals here with, among other items, the eight "filling" patterns (*ḥashw*) --- *fā'ilun*, *fā'ilātun*, etc. --- which serve to define and act as mnemonics for the prosodic meters. He immediately joins the eight musical meters "*al-thaqīl al-awwal*, *al-thaqīl al-thānī*, *mākhūrī*, *khafīf al-thaqīl*, *ramal*, *khafīf al-ramal*, *khafīf al-khafīf*, and *hazaj*" and says: "These eight basic forms (*ajnās*) [consist of] movements (*ḥarakāt*) and repose (*sukūn*) in a verse of poetry set to music (*mulaḥḥan*). They are [called] *asbāb* [sing. *sabab*], *fawāṣil* [sing. *fāṣila*], *awtād* [sing. *watid*], and *ghāyāt* [sing. *ghāya*]. *Sabab* is an 'attack' (*naqra*, i.e., the attack of the plectrum in plucking the strings of the lute) and a 'lifting' (*imsāk*, i.e., lifting of the plectrum). This [corresponds to] two consonants (*ḥarfān*), one [of them] followed by a vowel (*mutaḥarrik*), and [the other being] 'quiet' (*sākin*), such as [the syllables] *hal*, *bal*, [or] *qum*. They are identical (*yalzamuhu*) with [the syllable] *fa'* of the mnemotechnic syllables (*ḥashw*) used in poetry. The circle o is the sign of the *mutaḥarrik* consonant, and the stroke | is the symbol of the *sākin* consonant.... Hence *al-sabab al-khafīf* is [depicted by] o | . The second *sabab* is called *al-sabab al-thaqīl*, [it consists of syllables such as] *lama*, *nama*, *sama*, [and is depicted by] o o."[91]

Al-Kindī then explains the two *watids* (o o | and o | o), the *fāṣila* (o o o |), and the *ghāya* (o o o o |), using side by side the *'arūḍ* terms "*ḥarf mutaḥarrik*" and "*ḥarf sākin,*" and their equivalents in *īqā'*, *naqra* and *imsāk*, or *naqra* and *sukūn*. Consequently the *'arūḍ* pattern *fā'ilun* (o | o o |) becomes "one attack and a lifting [of the plectrum, followed by] two attacks and a lifting" (*naqra wa-imsāk wa-*

naqratān wa-imsāk). In the same way the remaining five of the eight *ḥashw* patterns are explained: *fa'ūlun* (o o | o |), *mafā'īlun* (o o | o | o |), *fā'ilātun* (o | o o | o |), and *mufā'alatun* (o o | o o o |).[92] But in contrast to all this, in the subsequent description of the eight *īqā'* "species," no reference is made to the previous terms and symbols. Al-Kindī turns abruptly to a distinctly different terminology. Right at the beginning of the definition of the first meter *al-thaqīl al-awwal,* a new term, "consecutive attacks" (*naqarāt mutawāliya*) is introduced without explanation, and the new term "silent attack" (*naqra sākina*) obviously denotes here a rest:

"As to the [eight] forms of *īqā'* (*ammā al-īqā'āt*): The first 'heavy' meter (*al-thaqīl al-awwal*) [consists of] three consecutive attacks (*naqarāt mutawāliya*), [followed by] a 'silent attack' (*naqra sākina*)." This description, as well as the following seven,[93] turn out to be more or less identical, essentially simplified versions of Isḥāq al-Mawṣilī's wordings transmitted by al-Fārābī[94] --- thus confirming al-Fārābī's statement that al-Kindī had borrowed his definitions of the *īqā'* forms from Isḥāq.[95] The above description corresponds to the base form (*aṣl*) of the meter *al-thaqīl al-awwal* as described also by other authors between the third century A.H./ninth century A.D. and the fifth century A.H./eleventh century A.D..[96] Transposed into modern musical notation, it equals three half notes and one half-note rest.

Had al-Kindī applied his initial theoretical outline to a description of *al-thaqīl al-awwal,* the result could have sounded like: "*al-thaqīl al-awwal* consists of three consecutive attacks of the kind of *al-sabab al-khafīf* (= *naqra* and *imsāk*), comparable to the pattern *maf'ūlun* and of a following rest corresponding to the length of one *sabab khafīf* (i.e., o | o | o | | |)." This application of the theory was apparently neither realized by al-Kindī's source(s) nor by himself. It is evident that he was dependent, in the theoretical part, on an *īqā'* theory derived from the science of *'arūḍ*. The existence of such theories is still attested in a passage by Ibn Nubāta al-Miṣrī (d. A.H. 768/A.D. 1366) in which he states that "people allege that the melodies (*alḥān*) are formed in accordance with prosodical meters (*mawḍū'a 'alā a'āriḍ*), but this is not true. Isḥāq al-Mawṣilī, the ultimate expert (*khātam al-qawm*), said: This was said by someone who is ignorant of this art."[97]

Al-Kindī seems to have been one of those worthy of this epithet and al-Fārābī's critique directed against his *īqā'* theory[98] turns out to be justified in this respect. In his eclecticism al-Kindī had combined theoretical bits of the "*'arūḍ-īqā'* theory" with Isḥāq's description of *īqā'* meters, without recognizing that they were incompatible.

For researchers, on the other hand, al-Kindī's naïveté is of great value in so far as it provides an intriguing clue as to what al-Khalīl (or any specialist in *'arūḍ* prior to al-Kindī) might have produced when he started out from the *'arūḍ* theory and embarked upon *īqā'*. A text such as that transmitted by al-Kindī could well have been written by a philologist interested in the metrical aspect of music without possessing a deeper insight into that art.

'Arūḍ theory is not transferable to *īqā'* in the straightforward way shown by al-Kindī, since the metrical phenomena differ in three essential aspects:

(1) In *'arūḍ*, a *ḥarf mutaḥarrik* and a *ḥarf sākin* are sufficiently explained by what is termed a "short" and a "long" syllable. Hence the basic pattern of the prosodic meter *ramal* was as correctly depicted by a pre-Khalīlian *lā na'am lā*[99] as by the Khalīlian *fā'ilātun*. In *īqā'*, on the other hand, a precise

relation between the values of the notes has to be fixed. The pre-Islamic or early Islamic mnemonics, *yā yadāh* or *yā hādiyāh,* used by musicians for *ḥudāʾ* songs,[100] do not, in the written form in which they are transmitted, convey the exact rhythm of the *īqāʿ* meter intended. In music theory, a *naqra* (or *ḥarf mutaḥarrik*) and a *sukūn* (or *ḥarf sākin*) have necessarily to be considered as elements of the same relative length, but of different absolute duration. With sufficient clarity this was exposed in al-Fārābī's *īqāʿ* theory.[101]

(2) *ʿArūḍ* theory can do with the above two elements, whereas *īqāʿ* is in need of the three components --- "short," "middle," and "long." This also was clearly exemplified by al-Fārābī.[102]

(3) The patterns of prosodic meters do not contain rests. The "rest" between *miṣrāʿ*s and *bayt*s have no prosodic function. But the rests between notes and between the "periods" (*adwār*, sing. *dawr*) of an *īqāʿ* are constitutive parts and have to be determined as "short," "middle," and "long," in analogy to the notes.[103]

The simple equation of *fāʿilātun* and the like with sequences of notes does not, therefore, correspond to the requirements of an adequate *īqāʿ* theory.

As it emerges from al-Kindī's text, the "*ʿarūḍ-īqāʿ* theory" of his time was not sufficiently developed to be applicable to the depiction of *īqāʿ* meters. It therefore may well have corresponded to the historical facts when in the *Ṭabaqāt al-mughannīn* a certain rudimental "depiction" (*rasm*) of *īqāʿ* was attributed to al-Khalīl, "to which could relate those who succeded him" in order to improve it. Although the main development of the *īqāʿ* theory from Isḥāq al-Mawṣilī to Abū Naṣr al-Fārābī and Ṣafī al-Dīn al-Urmawī (d. A.H.

693/A.D. 1294) and his followers was based upon different premises, the *fa'ala* patterns as well as the symbols used in *'arūḍ* were gradually integrated into the *īqā'* theory. But even in later times, the result was not always satisfying. The Ikhwān al-ṣafā', for example, followed al-Kindī rather closely in treating *'arūḍ* together with *īqā'* in their chapter on music, whereby they combined features of the "*'arūḍ-īqā'* theory" with those of al-Fārābī's *īqā'* system.[104] They even give the helpful ratio of *ḥaraka* : *sabab* : *watid* : *fāṣila* = 1 : 2 : 3 : 4 to serve as a means for defining the length of notes.[105] But when describing the form *al-thaqīl al-awwal* (which slightly differs from that given by al-Kindī) and the other meters, they are unable to apply this method.[106] The problem of the rests was likewise not solved by them, and it continued to exist in later sources, mainly those written by men of letters or philologists. In Ibn al-Sīd al-Baṭalyawsī's (d. A.H. 521/A.D. 1127) commentary on Abū al-'Alā' al-Ma'arrī's *Siqṭ al-zand* the three ("heavy") attacks of *al-thaqīl al-awwal* are correctly expressed by *maf'ūlun*, but the following rest is tacitly omitted.[107] On the other hand, Ibn Zayla (d. 440/1048), a pupil of Ibn Sīnā, was a writer on music theory, who successfully combined elements of al-Fārābī's *īqā'* theory with those of *'arūḍ*. He used the symbols *tā'* for attack and o for duration and rest, and thus gave an unmistakable depiction of *al-thaqīl al-awwal*, namely: ت o | ت o | ت o | o o.[108]

Because of the scarce remains of Isḥāq al-Mawṣilī's literary heritage in music theory, no evidence for his dependance on and further development of al-Khalīl's theoretical attempts as postulated in the *Ṭabaqāt al-mughannīn* could be evidenced in the above pages. On the contrary, Isḥāq's extant texts convey a distinctively individual view on the material and a personal style in dealing with it, be it in the realm of *nagham* or of *īqā'*. This leads to the conclusion that whatever al-Khalīl has contributed to these disciplines was either tacitly absorbed (and changed) in the writings of Isḥāq, or remained unnoticed, except for the first indications of an "*ʿarūḍ-īqāʿ* theory" traceable in al-Kindī's *Kitāb al-muṣawwitāt al-watariyya*. This can be regarded as an indirect indication of al-Khalīl's activities in music theory and may, indeed, have gone back to the *Kitāb al-īqāʿ* of the great philologist.

Note added in May 1996:

The manuscript was submitted in August 1990. A revised and enlarged German version ("Al-Ḫalīl ibn Aḥmad und die Frügeschichte der arabischen Lehre von den 'Tönen' und den musikalischen Metren") appears in *Zeitschrift für Geschichte der arabisch-islamischen Wissenschaften* (Frankfurt), vol. 10 (1995/96). E.N

Notes

1. Cf. C. Brockelmann, *Geschichte der arabischen Litteratur*, Suppl. vol 1 (Leiden, 1937), 159: "Er ist der eigentliche Begründer der arabischen Grammatik,...der Lexikographie und der Metrik."

2. See F. Sezgin, *Geschichte des arabischen Schrifttums*, vol. 9 (Leiden, 1984), 46-47.

3. Ibid., vol. 8 (Leiden, 1982), 52-56.

4. According to S. Wild, *Das Kitāb al-ʿAin und die arabische Lexikographie* (Wiesbaden, 1965), 37-40.

5. See Abū al-Rayḥān al-Bīrūnī, *Kitāb fī taḥqīq mā li-l-hind* (Haydarabad, A.H. 1377/A.D. 1958), 115; and E.C. Sachau, *Alberuni's India*, vol. 1 (London, 1888), 197-198.

6. Cf. G. Weil, "ʿArūḍ," in *Encyclopaedia of Islam*, 2d. ed. vol. 1 (Leiden, London, 1960), 667-677; W. Heinrichs, "Metrik," in *Grundriss der arabischen Philologie*, vol.2, *Literaturwissenschaft* (Wiesbaden, 1987), 190-200.

7. First pointed out by R. Sellheim in his article on al-Khalīl in *The*

Encyclopaedia of Islam, 2d.ed., vol. 4 (Leiden, 1978), 962.

8. G. Flügel, ed. (Leipzig, 1871-72), 43.

9. A pioneering study on al-Khalīl's musical activities was written by ʻAlī al-Zubaydī, "*al-Khalīl al-mūsīqār*," *al-Mawrid*, vol. 4, part 4 (Baghdad, A.H. 1395/A.D. 1975), 23-29. Al-Zubaydī was the first to make known the important passage by al-Kindī in which elements of *ʻarūḍ* and *īqāʻ* are brought together, and which is discussed below. However, in interpreting this and other sources related to al-Khalīl and music, our results differ. Al-Zubaydī repeats in his article (1975:25) the assumption of H.G. Farmer that "probably it was al-Khalīl's theories that Ibn Firnās (d. A.H. 274/A.D.887) introduced into Spain," expressed in his contribution on "Music" in *The Legacy of Islam*, ed. Th. Arnold and A. Guillaume, (Oxford; London, 1931), 356-375, here page 363; repr. in *Studies in Oriental Music*, vol.1(Frankfurt, 1986), 129-150, here page 137. This could not be confirmed.

10. Latest edition by ʻAbd al-Salām M. Hārūn in *Rasāʼil al- Jāḥiẓ*, vol. 3 (Cairo, A.H. 1399/A.D. 1979), 129-136.

11. The text is corrupt. My additions are in square brackets.

12. Pages 131-132 in the edition of ʻAbd al-Salām M. Hārūn.

13. See al-Jāḥiẓ, *Kitāb al-ḥayawān*, ed. ʻAbd al-Salām M. Hārūn, vol.7 (Cairo, A.H. 1364/A.D. 1945), 165-166.

14. Ibid., vol.1 (Cairo, A.H. 1356/A.D. 1938), 150.

15. *al-Mukhtār min al-muqtabas* by ʻAlī ibn Ḥasan ibn Muʻāwiya, facsimile edition by F. Sezgin et al. (Frankfurt, 1990), 185.

16. *al-Tanbīh ʻalā ḥudūth al-taṣḥīf*, ed. M. Asʻad Ṭalas (Damascus, A.H. 1388/A.D. 1968), 120.

17. *Simṭ al-laʼālī*, ed. ʻAbd al-ʻAzīz al-Maymanī (Cairo, A.H. 1354/A.D. 1936), 815.

18. *Ṭabaqāt al-naḥwiyyīn wa-l-lughawiyyīn*, ed. M. Abū al-Faḍl Ibrāhīm, 2d. ed. (Cairo, 1973), 49; cf. *al-Mukhtār min al-muqtabas* (note 15), 187.

19. See Ibn Khurradādhbih, *Mukhtār min kitāb al-lahw wa-l-malāhī*, ed. A. ʻAbduh Khalīfa (Beirut, [1961]), 40-43; H.G. Farmer, *A History of Arabian Music to the XIIIth Century* (London, 1929), 83-84.

20. G. Flügel, ed. (Leipzig, 1871-72), 145.

21. Ibid.

22. Abū al-Faraj al-Iṣfahānī, *Kitāb al-aghānī al-kabīr*, vol. 4 (Cairo, A.H. 1369/A.D. 1950), 398. In the following, this Cairo edition (1927ff.) will be quoted under the title *Kitāb al-aghānī.*

23. Ibn Khurradādhbih, *op.cit.* (note 19), 41.

24. G. Flügel, ed. (Leipzig, 1871-72), 43.

25. *Irshād al-arīb*, ed. D.S. Margoliouth, vol. 4 (London, 1927), 182; *Mu'jam al-udabā'*, ed. A. Farīd Rifā'ī, vol. 2 (Cairo, A.H. 1356/A.D. 1937), 74, 75.

26. Cf. 'Alī ibn Yūsuf al-Qifṭī, *Inbāh al-ruwāt 'alā anbāh al-nuḥāt*, ed. M. Abū al-Faḍl Ibrāhīm, vol. 1 (Cairo, A.H. 1369/A.D. 1950), 343 (*Kitāb al-īqā'*); Ibn Khallikān, *Kitāb wafayāt al-a'yān wa-abnā' al-zamān*, vol. 1 (Būlāq, A.H. 1299), 217 (*Kitāb al-nagham)*; Ḥājjī Khalīfa, *Kashf al-ẓunūn*, ed. Şerefettin Yaltkaya, Kilisli Rıfat Bilge, vol. 2 (Istanbul, 1943), col. 1467 (*Kitāb al-nagham*).

27. *al-Tanbīh 'alā ḥudūth al-taṣḥīf* (note 16), 120.

28. *Simṭ al-la'ālī* (note 17), 815.

29. *Rasā'il al-Jāḥiẓ*, ed. 'Abd al-Salām M. Hārūn, vol. 3 (Cairo, A.H. 1399/A.D. 1979), 132.

30. *Kitāb al-ḥayawān*, ed. 'Abd al-Salām M. Hārūn, vol. 1 (Cairo, 1356/1938), 150.

31. *Ta'rīkh al-'ulamā' al-naḥwiyyīn*, ed. 'Abd al- Fattāḥ M. al-Ḥilw (Riyadh, A.H. 1401/A.D. 1981), 132.

32. *Ṭabaqāt al-shu'arā' al-muḥdathīn*, ed. 'Abbās Iqbāl (London, 1939), 38.

33. *al-Mukhtār min al-muqtabas* (note 15), 146.

34. M. Bahjat al-Atharī, ed. in *Majallāt al-Majma' al-'ilmiyy al-'irāqiyy* vol. 1 (Bagdad, A.H. 1369/A.D. 1950), 113-124; ed. Zakariyyā Yūsuf under the misleading title *Risālat Yaḥyā ibn al-Munajjim fī l-mūsīqā* (Cairo, 1964), (the correct title, *Kitāb al-nagham*, is cited in *Kitāb al-aghānī*, vol. 8, 374); study by O. Wright, "Ibn al-Munajjim and the Early Arabian Modes," in *The Galpin Society Journal*, 19 (1966), 27-48; facsimile edition and study by Yūsuf Shawqī, *Risālat Ibn al-Munajjim fī l-mūsīqā wa-kashf rumūz kitāb al-aghānī* (Cairo, 1976).

35. H.G. Farmer, *The Sources of Arabian Music*. 2d. ed. (Leiden, 1965), 10, no. 58.

36. Vol. 5, 270-405 passim.

37. *Kitāb al-nagham*, ed. al-Atharī (note 34), 116-119.

38. Ibid., 116; *Kitāb al-aghānī*, 8:373 (here, misleadingly, *al-nagham al-'ashr*).

39. *Kitāb al-nagham*, ed. al-Atharī (note 34), 116.

40. Ibid., 120-122; cf. *Kitāb al-aghānī*, 5:270.

41. See *Kitāb al-aghānī,* 8:374.

42. Ed. al-Atharī (note 34), 122-124.

43. Cf. *Kitāb al-aghānī,* 8:374.

44. *Jawāhir al-niẓām fī ma'rifat al-anghām*, written by Shams al-Dīn Abū 'Abd Allah Muḥammad ibn 'Alī ibn al-Khaṭīb al-Irbilī (see A. Shiloah, *The Theory of Music in Arabic Writings* (Munich, 1979), no. 168).

45. Cf. E. Werner, "The Origin of the Eight Modes of Music," in *Hebrew Union College Annual* 21 (Cincinnati, 1948) 211-255.

46. Ibn al-Ṭaḥḥān, *Ḥāwī al-funūn wa-salwat al-maḥzūn*, facsimile edition (Frankfurt, 1990), 199. This confirms M. Ullmann's observation that the musical connotations of the word *laḥn* came from the Greek, but it contradicts his assertion that they first appeared in the third century A.H. (ninth A.D.). See his *Wa-khayru l-ḥadīthi mā kāna laḥnan, Beiträge zur Lexikographie des Klassischen Arabisch,* no.1 (Munich, 1979), 15-17.

47. For the title see F. Sezgin, *Geschichte des arabischen Schrifttums*, vol.1 (Leiden, 1967), 270. The *Kitāb al-luḥūn al-thamāniya* is mentioned by Ibn 'Abd Rabbihi in *al-'Iqd al-farīd* ed. A. Amīn et al; vol. 6 (Cairo, A.H. 1368/A.D. 1949), 27.

48. See Zakariyyā Yūsuf, ed., *Mu'allafāt al-Kindī al- mūsīqiyya* (Baghdad, 1962), 54-57; R. Lachmann, Maḥmūd el-Hifnī, ed. and trans., *Ya'qūb ibn Isḥāq al-Kindī: Risāla fī khubr ta'līf al-alḥān* (Leipzig, 1931), xiii-xiv.

49. Mentioned by al-Kindī in the same text, page 52 (ed. Z. Yūsuf); page xi, (ed. Lachmann/Hifnī).

50. Ibid., 57 (ed. Z. Yūsuf); xiv, (ed. Lachmann/Hifnī).

51. Their relationship is indicated by al-Kindī in his *Risāla fī l-luḥūn wa-l-nagham*, ed. Zakariyyā Yūsuf (Baghdad, 1965), 26. Cf. *Mu'allafāt al-Kindī al-mūsīqiyya* (note 48), 137.

52. *Kitāb al-aghānī,* 3:276.

53. See Ibn Khurradādhbih, *Mukhtār min kitāb al-lahw wa-l-malāhī* (note 19), 15, line 6-7 (read *al-ṭurūq* instead of *al-kurūf*).

54. Cf. H.G. Farmer, "The Old Persian Musical Modes," *Journal of the Royal Asiatic Society* (1926), 93-95, repr. in H.G. Farmer, *Studies in Oriental Music, vol. 1.*

55. (Frankfurt, 1986), 426-428, esp. 426.

56. The term *rāh* was still used synonymously with the term *ṭarīq [sic]* in the music chapter of the *Qābūsnāma*, written in A.H. 475/A.D. 1082 by 'Unṣur al-Ma'ālī Kaykā'ūs ibn Iskandar ibn Qābūs ibn Wushmagīr, latest edition by Ghulām Ḥusayn Yūsufī (Teheran, 1362h (*shamsī*)/1983), 232-

239, esp. 233.

57. This was emphasized by A. Shiloah in the introduction of his translation of al-Ḥasan ibn Aḥmad ibn ʻAlī al-Kātib, *La perfection des connaissances musicales* (*Kamāl adab al-ghināʼ*) (Paris, 1972), 18, lines 13-15.

58. See *Mukhtār min kitāb al-lahw wa-l-malāhī* (note 19), passim.

59. *Ashʻār awlād al-khulafāʼ*, ed. J. Heyworth-Dunne (Cairo, 1936), 5 and passim.

60. Ibid., 4.

61. Ibid., 31.

62. Ibid., 60 and passim.

63. Al-Kindi equates as national or regional systems the eight meters of *īqāʻ* (*madhhab al-ʻarab*) with the *oktōēchos* (*madhhab al-rūm*) and the Iranian *ṭuruq* [sic,] (*madhhab al-furs*), see *Muʼallafāt al-Kindī al-mūsīqiyya* (note 48), 137.

64. *Ḥāwī al-funūn* (note 46), 180, 213-214; al-Ḥasan ibn Aḥmad ibn ʻAlī al-Kātib, *Kamāl adab al-ghināʼ*, ed. Zakariyyā Yūsuf, *al-Mawrid* (Baghdad, 1973), 2:101-154, esp. 142, French trans. by A. Shiloah (note 57), 159.

65. Formed in analogy to *ramal maḥmūl* (*Ḥāwī al-funūn*, 203), *al-ramal al-muʻallaq* (ibid., 204), *al-ramal al-munsariḥ* (ibid., 205), and *al-ramal al-maḥṣūr* (ibid., 206).

66. *Kitāb al-aghānī*, 15:381.

67. Ibid., 1:4-5; cf. H.G. Farmer, "The Song Captions in the Kitāb al-Aghānī al-Kabīr," *Transactions of the Glasgow University Oriental Society*, 15 (1953-54), 1-10; repr. in *Studies in Oriental Music* (Frankfurt, 1986), 433-442.

68. Cf. the six "old" mode names (*aṣābiʻ* !) *muṭlaq*, *muʻallaq*, *maḥmūl*, *munsariḥ*, *mazmūm*, and *mujannab* in Ibn Faḍl Allāh al-ʻUmarī, *Masālik al-abṣār fī mamālik al-amṣār*, facsimile edition by F. Sezgin et al., vol. 10 (Frankfurt, 1988), 3.

69. *Al-muṭlaq*, *al-mazmūm*, *al-khusrawānī*, and *al-mujannab* are attested for being current in *al-Andalus* by Aḥmad ibn Yūsuf al-Tīfāshī (d. A.H. 651/A.D. 1253) in his *Mutʻat al-asmāʻ fī ʻilm al-samāʻ*, see M. ibn Tāwīt al-Ṭanjī, "*al-Ṭarāʼiq wa-l-alḥān al-mūsīqiyya fī ifrīqiyya wa-l-andalus*," *al-Abḥāth* (Beirut, 1968), 21: 93-116, esp. 115.

70. Ibn Khurradādhbih, op. cit. (note 19), 41.

71. A well-known transmitter of Yūnus' book who added the *ṭarīqa* indications (see *Kitāb al-aghānī,* 12:126) was a certain al-Hishāmī (third century A.H./ninth century A.D.). He played an important part in the transmission of song books and was frequently quoted by Abū al-Faraj al-Iṣfahāni. The latter also found material from Yūnus' book in the song books of Aḥmad ibn Yaḥyā al-Makkī (d. A.H. 248/A.D. 862), and ʻAmr ibn Bāna (d. A.H. 278/A.D. 891) (see *Kitāb al-aghānī,* 3:322-323). In the version of Yūnus' book used by ibn Khurradādhbih (note 19), the *ṭarīqa* indications were still reduced to the meter without mention of the mode.

72. This becomes apparent from the book titles and text fragments of Isḥāq al-Mawṣilī and from the extant work of al-Kindī.

73. Ibn Khurradādhbih, op. cit. (note 19), 55.

74. See Yāqūt al-Ḥamawī, *Muʻjam al-udabāʼ* (note 25), 11:73-74; Ibn al-Qifṭī, *Inbāh al-ruwāt* (note 26), 1: 343; Ibn Khallikān, *Wafayāt al-aʻyān* (note 26), 1:216; Jalāl al-Dīn al-Suyūṭī, *Bughyat al-wuʻāt fī ṭabaqāt al-lughawiyyīn wa-l-nuḥāt*, ed. M. Abū al-Faḍl Ibrāhīm, vol. 1 (Cairo, A.H. 1348/A.D. 1964), 558; O. Rescher, *Abriss der arabischen Litteraturgeschichte*, vol. 2 (Stuttgart, 1933), 199.

75. The legend of the inspiring beats of the coppersmiths was not only related to Pythagoras, but also to al-Khalīl; see *al-Mukhtār min al-muqtabas* (note 94), 146; cf. W. Heinrichs, "Metrik" (note 85), 199.

76. For the practical side of their relationship, see O. Wright, "Music and Verse," in *Arabic Literature to the End of the Umayyad Period*, ed. A.F.L. Beeston et al., The Cambridge History of Arabic Literature (Cambridge, 1983), 433-459.

77. *Kitāb al-aghānī,* 1:315.

78. Ibid., 5:230 and 6:283; cf. O. Wright, op. cit. (note 76), 459. *Ramal* and *hazaj* are common to both *ʻarūḍ* and *īqāʻ*. In a future discussion of the early development of the two disciplines and their interdependence, these two meters will play a principal part. But it will also be of interest to consider why *rajaz* has *not* become an *īqāʻ* meter. First steps in this direction were taken by O. Wright, op. cit. (note 76); cf. W. Heinrichs (note 6), 192.

79. The six "old" meters *al-thaqīl al-awwal*, *al-thaqīl al-thānī, khafīf al-thaqīl*, *ramal*, *khafīf al-ramal*, and *hazaj* are listed by Ibn Faḍl Allāh al-ʻUmarī in *Masālik al-abṣār* (note 68), 10:2-3; cf. H.G. Farmer, *A History of Arabian Music* (note 19), 71. The seven meters *hazaj*, *khafīf al-ramal, (thaqīl al-) ramal*, *al-thaqīl al-thānī, kafīf al-thaqīl al-thānī (= al-mākhūrī)*, *al-thaqīl al-awwal*, and *khafīf al-thaqīl al-awwal* are described in the *Mafātīḥ al-ʻulūm*, ed. G. van Vloten, (Leiden, 1895), 245-246, English transl. by H.G. Farmer, "The Science of Music in the *Mafātīḥ al-'ulūm*," *Transactions of the Glasgow University Oriental Society*, 17 (1957-58),1-9, here 8-9; repr. in *Studies in Oriental Music* (Frankfurt, 1986), 1:453-461, here 460-461. Seven meters are also mentioned by al-Ḥasan ibn Aḥmad 'Alī al-Kātib in his *Kamāl adab al-ghinā'*, Arabic text (note 64) 137, French trans. (note 57), 144: *ramal, al-thaqīl al-awwal, al-thaqīl al-thānī,* and their *khafīf* forms, and *hazaj*.

80. *Mukhtār min kitāb al-lahw wa-l-malāhī* (note 19), 55.

81. *Kitāb al-aghānī,* 6:283; Ibn al-Ṭaḥḥān: *Ḥāwī al-funūn* (note 46), 202.

82. *Kamāl adab al-ghinā',* Arabic text (note 64), 138, French trans. (note 57), 165.

83. See Abū Bakr al-Ṣūlī, *Ash'ār awlād al-khulafā'* (note 59), 23; *Kitāb al-aghānī,* 1:5; Ibn al-Ṭaḥḥān, *Ḥāwī al-funūn* (note 46), 199-200.

84. *Kitāb al-aghānī,* 10:278.

85. Ibid., 23:148.

86. Ibid., 1:96; 16:359; 19:73, 303.

87. Ibid., 19:76.

88. *al-'Ayn*, ed. Mahdī al-Makhzūmī and Ibrāhīm al-Samarrā'ī, vol. 8 (Qum, Iran, n.d.), 267.

89. Ibid., 3:385.

90. MS Manisa (Turkey), 1705, fol. 59a-89b, esp. 79b-81b.

91. *Kitāb al-muṣawwitāt al-watariyya min dhāt al-watar al-wāḥid ilā dhāt al-'asharat al-awtār*, in *Mu'allafāt al-Kindī al-mūsīqiyya* (note 48), 69-92, esp. 80-82.

92. Ibid., 80-81.

93. Ibid., 81-82.

94. *al-thaqīl al-thānī, al-mākhūrī, khafīf al-thaqīl, al-ramal, khafīf al-ramal, khafīf al-khafīf, al-hazaj.*

95. In *Kitāb iḥṣā' al-īqā'at* (note 90), fol. 80a-81b, in the following order: *al-khafīf, al-hazaj, al-ramal al-khafīf, al-ramal al-thaqīl, khafīf al-thaqīl al-awwal, al-thaqīl al-awwal, khafīf al-thaqīl al-thānī, al-thaqīl al-thānī.*

96. Ibid., fol. 81b.

97. For al-Kindī and others, see H.G. Farmer, *Sa'adyah Gaon on the Influence of Music* (London, 1943), 79. For al-Fārābī see G.D. Sawa, *Music Performance Practice in the Early 'Abbāsid Era 132-A.H. 320/A.D. 750-932* (Toronto, 1989), 42. For al-Ḥasan ibn Aḥmad al-Kātib and others, see A. Shiloah, *La perfection des connaissances musicales* (note 57), 145.

98. *Sarḥ al-ʿuyūn fī sharḥ risālat ibn Zaydūn*, ed. M. Abū al-Faḍl Ibrāhīm (Cairo, A.H. 1383/196), 235.

99. See *Kitāb iḥṣāʾ al-īqāʿāt* (note 90), fol. 181b, 88a-b.

100. See W. Heinrichs, "Metrik" (note 6), 192-193, note 29.

101. See al-Masʿūdī, *Murūj al-dhahab*, ed. C. Barbier de Meynard, vol. 8 (Paris, 1874), 92; cf. Ibn Khurradādhbih, *Mukhtār min kitāb al-lahw wa-l-malāhī* (note 34), 18.

102. See G.D. Sawa, op. cit. (note 96), 38.

103. Ibid., 38; 41-45.

104. Ibid., 39.

105. *Rasāʾil Ikhwān al-ṣafāʾ wa-khullān al-wafāʾ*, vol. 1 (Beirut:Dar Ṣādir A.H. 1376/A.D. 1957), 196-202; French trans. by A. Shiloah in *Revue des Études Islamiques* (Paris, 1964), 32: 142-148.

106. Ibid., Arabic text 199; French trans. 145.

107. Ibid., Arabic text 227; French trans. in *Revue des Études Islamiques* 34 (1966), 176-177.

108. *Shurūḥ siqṭ al-zand*, ed. Muṣṭafā al-Saqqā et al. , vol. 3 (Cairo, A.H. 1366/A.D. 1947), 1189.

109. *Al-Kāfī fī l-mūsīqī*, ed. Zakariyyā Yūsuf (Cairo, 1964), 62.

Aspects of the Genitive: Taxonomy in *al-Jumal fī al-naḥw*

Karin C. Ryding

Introduction

This article is in two parts. The first section is a discussion of and description of *al-Jumal fī al-naḥw*, an early Arabic treatise on morphosyntax attributed to al-Khalīl ibn Aḥmad. The second part is an annotated translation of the section on the genitive, which is the third section in the treatise.

The Text and the Topic

Al-Jumal fī al-naḥw (henceforth, *Jumal*), "The Totalities of Syntax,"[1] is an early medieval study of morphosyntactic categories as reflected in the dimensions of classical Arabic desinential inflection, or *iʿrāb*: case markers on substantives and mood markers on imperfective verbs. This syntactically governed morphological category is distinct in Arabic linguistic theory from other types of inflection (i.e., for number or gender) and constitutes a key theoretical issue in medieval Arabic linguistics.[2] Part of this distinction lies in the syncretism or fusing of categories of desinential inflection across form class boundaries.

Case/mood inflection appears to have become largely redundant in spoken Arabic by the post-Islamic period and was among the first features of the old (classical) language to be shed in its drift towards vernacular.[3] Nevertheless, knowledge of desinential inflection maintained a kind of elitist appeal as an intellectual challenge, as well as being a *sine qua non* for exegesis of scripture.

This particular text is an excellent example of the early elaboration of Arabic grammatical taxonomic systems and practice, that is, the distinguishing, ordering and labeling of type groups within the subject field, along with attestations and examples of all categories specified in the analysis.[4] Its importance lies not only in its content and methodology, but also in the fact that it is attributed to lexicographer, grammarian, and teacher al-Khalīl ibn Aḥmad (d. ca. A.H. 175/A.D. 791). Even if its composition dates back not to al-Khalīl in the late eighth century, but only to the late ninth or early tenth centuries, it remains a significant historical document in its scope, structure, and methods of analysis.

One assumes that many Arabic grammatical issues had been discussed, researched, and settled by the second half of the eighth century, but that they had not been organized or codified, and the status of grammatical theory was rudimentary. Reuschel, in his seminal study of al-Khalīl, remarks that by the time of Sībawayh (d. ca. A.H. 180/A.D. 796), the groundwork had been done, but he believes that al-Khalīl was a major theoretician and made fundamental contributions to the development and elaboration of Arabic grammatical theory.[5]

The *Jumal* text is a taxonomy of categories of desinential inflection (*al-iʿrāb*), distinguishing, ordering, and naming all types of occurrences of *rafʿ* (nominative/indicative), *naṣb* (accusative/ subjunctive), *khafḍ* (genitive /epenthetic), and *jazm* (apocopate). It illustrates the degree to which case/mood syncretism existed in early Arabic linguistic theory, juxtaposing case and mood in ways that are unfamiliar to Western linguists, but which have a rationale, integrity, and coherence of their own. The theoretical framework for the presentation of these categories is founded on the concepts of documentation, explanation, and coverage of the full range of Arabic morphosyntactic features. If there is one salient feature of the text, it is its exhaustive coverage of categories (*wujūh*) of desinence.[6]

Aside from its comprehensiveness, the documentation of occurring categories is scrupulously based on a wide-ranging body of attested examples of three kinds:[7]

1. Citations from the Qurʾān,
2. Citations from pre-Islamic and early Islamic poetry, and
3. Examples created by the author to illustrate spoken Arabic usage.[8]

Meticulous attestation is provided for every type group distinguished and constitutes a wealth of evidence upon which to base Arabic morphosyntactic theory. An intriguing aspect of certain Qurʾānic citations is that they seem to be variants of the canonical standard and are cause for interesting attempts at analysis. In most cases, however, the author notes when there is debate among Qurʾānic readers/reciters on a particular point of morphosyntax.

The parameters of inquiry and discussion are not limited strictly to categories of case and mood usage. Approximately the last third of the text is devoted to analysis and classification of the occurrences of function morphemes, some of which are free and some bound, but most of which consist of one consonant phoneme or letter. This includes the twenty-two aspects of *alif* (which covers both the vowel *ā* and the word-initial glottal stop), the thirty aspects of *lām*, the ten aspects of *hāʾ*, the fifteen aspects of *tāʾ*, the ten aspects of *wāw*, the thirteen aspects of *lām-alif* (including *illā*, "except for"), and the ten aspects of *mā*. In a postscript are appended the seven aspects of *fāʾ*,

the ten aspects of *nūn*, the four aspects of *bā'*, the nine aspects of *yā'*, a discussion of the term *ruwayda*, "slowly," and the difference between *am* and *aw*, two types of disjunctive coordinators.

The Genitive: *al-khafḍ*

The chapter on the genitive inflection is considerably shorter than the first two chapters, which deal respectively with the accusative/subjunctive and the nominative/indicative. This is because the genitive or *kasra*-marker is substantive-specific, and is not used as a mood marker on verbs, as the *fatḥa* and *ḍamma* are. The author consistently uses the term *khafḍ* "depression" to denote both syntactically determined and non-syntactically determined substantive suffixes, including both the category of genitive case-marker and the fixed low-front vowel ending on indeclinable nouns and adjectives (e.g., the invariable *-i* suffix on the term *ams-i*, "yesterday"). Terminologically, therefore, this text differs from Sībawayh's, inasmuch as the latter uses primarily the term *jarr,* "pulling," for genitive.

It agrees partially, however, with the description of al-Khalīl's terminology provided by al-Khwārizmī in his tenth century encyclopedia, *Mafātīḥ al-'ulūm*, "The Keys to the Sciences." In the chapter on grammar, in the section dealing in particular with al-Khalīl, al-Khwārizmī defines his usage of the term *khafḍ* as "what occurs at the end of a nunated word such as *zayd-in*."[9] In the same passage, al-Khwārizmī states that al-Khalīl uses the term *kasr* to refer to "what occurs at the end of a non-nunated word, such as the *lām* of *al-jamal-i* (the camel)"; and he lists the term *jarr* as referring to "what occurs at the end of jussive (apocopate) verbs when they encounter *alif al-waṣl*, such as *lam yadhhab-i l-rajul*."[10] Thus, according to this author, al-Khalīl's use of *kasr* would refer to any non-nunated word ending, whereas *jarr* would be restricted to epenthetic or "helping" vowels. As pointed out by Fischer in his article about al-Khwārizmī's chapter on grammar,

> Sībawayh rejected al-Khalīl's term *khafḍ,* "depression or lowering," in spite of its apparent correspondence to *naṣb*, "erection or placing," and *raf'*, "elevation or lifting." Obviously he had a different concept of the genitive case, when he chose *jarr,* "traction," as the appropriate technical term. He had got the idea of grammatical annexation, according to which the annexing word (*jarr*, "drawing") "draws" the annexed one (*majrūr,* "drawn"), i.e., the genitive. Al-Khalīl knew *jarr* as a linguistic term also, but with a very different meaning; in his system *jarr* did not have any syntactic content, it describes *i* at the end of a word as a merely phonetic phenomenon, which "draws" the following word, if it begins with *alif al-waṣl.* [11]

In fact, in the *Jumal* text, the term *jarr* is used only once, as a substitute for the term *khafḍ* in a chapter title.[12] For non-genitive inflection expressed as *-i*, the lexical root *k-s-r* is used. *Khafḍ* predominates, but not where the reference is to inflection of a non-substantive. Referring both to the *i* on the word *inna* and to the *i* on the feminine singular past tense marker of the verb, al-Khalīl uses *k-s-r*, e.g., "*kusirat-i l-alif*" (on *inna,* p. 188); "*kasar-ta al-tā'*" (in *anti kharaj-ti*, p. 278). Moreover, *k-s-r* is also used to denote the insertion of the helping vowel after the feminine singular third person past tense verb suffix. In an interesting passage from the section on the various kinds of *tā'*, the author states:

kharajat-i-l-mar'at-u. kasar-ta al-tā', li-l-tiqā' al-sākinayn. wa l-sākināni: al-tā' min "kharaj-at" wa l-lām min "l-mar'a." wa kull-u majzūm-in wa sākin-in idhā ḥurrika ḥurrika ilā al-khafḍ."[13]

(In the sentence) "the woman went out," you put *kasra* on the *ta'* because of the meeting of two quiescent (non-voweled) consonants. The two consonants are the *ta'* of *kharajat* and the *lām* of *l-mar'a*. Every jussive (apocopate) and quiescent consonant, when it is voweled, is voweled like the genitive.

This passage provides a distinction between the use of *k-s-r* and the use of *kh-f-ḍ*. I think it is clear that the preposition *ilā* in the last line is used in the meaning of "like" (as in the expression *wa mā ilayhi*, "and the like").

Further distinction can be drawn on the basis of the *Jumal*'s description of the "markers" (*'alāmāt*) of the genitive (*al-khafḍ*)[14] where there is an explicit listing of *kasra*, *yā'*, and *fatḥa* as those markers. The fact that *kasra* is the "unmarked" or base form of the genitive suffix leads to most of the confusion.

Thus, the *Jumal* text agrees partially with al-Khwārizmī's listing of al-Khalīl's terms, but not fully. The agreement on the term *khafḍ*, is important, however, because this term has been considered more characteristic of the Kufan school of Arabic grammar than the Basran school.[15] If there is evidence that the term can be attributed to al-Khalīl, this supports the argument for attributing the *Jumal* text to him.

Editions Consulted

As the basis for the translation of the chapter on the genitive,

I examined two versions of the text. One version was edited and annotated by Fakhr al-Dīn Qabāwa, and published under the title *al-Jumal fī al-naḥw* in 1985 in Beirut. It is based on comparison of three manuscripts, one from the Aya Sofya Library in Istanbul, dated A.H. 601 (A.D. 1204); another from the Qawala Library in Dār al-Kutub in Cairo, dated A.H. 722 (A.D. 1324); and a third from the Beşir Âğa Library in Istanbul, dated A.H. 865 (A.D. 1466).

The Aya Sofya copy was selected by Qabāwa as the "base" manuscript because of its accuracy and completeness as well as its being the oldest. The others, referred to by Qabāwa as manuscripts "Q" and "B," respectively, are used for comparison and supplementation. Whereas the base copy and manuscript "B" are attributed solely to al-Khalīl ibn Aḥmad on their title pages, manuscript "Q," in Cairo, is attributed both to al-Khalīl and to Baghdadi grammarian Abū Bakr ʿAbdallāh ibn Muḥammad ibn Shuqayr (d. A.H. 317/A.D. 929). Qabāwa presents a strong case in his introduction for attributing authorship to al-Khalīl ibn Aḥmad.

However, the Qawala (Cairo) version was subsequently published in 1987, edited by Fāʾiz Fāris, entitled *al-Muḥallā* and attributed by the editor to Ibn Shuqayr.[16] Fāris uses the Qawala manuscript as his base version and compares it with the Aya Sofya text. Thus two edited versions of this manuscript exist in Arabic today, ascribed to different authors. Each editor prefaces his edition with an extensive analysis of sources and discussion of the rationale behind the determination of attribution. I examined both versions of the text and both editorial introductions in order to weigh their relative merit. It was apparent that both editors had done extensive research on the topic of authorship, but Qabāwa's analysis seemed both more objective and exhaustive.

Fāris is very clear in his introduction that the most important thing for him to establish is that al-Khalīl is definitely not the author of this manuscript. It is less important to him to prove who the author really is, but he favors Ibn Shuqayr.[17] He lists six reasons to doubt al-Khalīl's authorship, among them the fact that Kufan terminology is used in the book. But he does not go into discussion of the terminology or cite examples. He also maintains that the opening line of the manuscript, "al-Khalīl ibn Aḥmad said"... "does not necessarily mean that the author is al-Khalīl" since this kind of opening is used in "other books," but again, he does not provide examples.[18] Fāris, although acknowledging this opening line in his introduction, actually omits it from his published version of the manuscript.

Qabāwa believes the text is attributable to al-Khalīl "in its strange and distinctive sectioning, its divisions, orientation, judgments, sayings and terminology," and that its "special framework .... represents an archaic stage of the understanding of the meanings of grammar, its parts and its wholes, and the relation of each one with what surrounds it."[19]

He readily admits, however, that there is variation, particularly in quality:

> It includes in its design texts, expressions and citations which are undoubtedly inserted, added in by scholars, scribes or readers after al-Khalīl, that got mixed into the original, and were handed down by copyists as though they were part of it, at the same time that it contains examples that were known in the school of al-Khalīl and his sayings, or what he himself knew about.

It first and last shows different levels in thought, plan, and expression. While you are tautly focused on the precision of

> delineations, the depth of thought, the clarity of meaning, the extent of vision, the broadness of the horizon, the skill in reasoning, the firmness of production, then you are surprised by the phenomena of disorganization, intrusion, and absurdities. While you are taken by the perfectly precise definitions, wise, guiding qualifications and judgments, and vivid, pertinent opinions, then you collide with fragments of pompous, generalized, superficial definitions, and limited, ineffective judgments. While succumbing to the elegance of language, the clarity of expression, the soundness of texture, the precision of rendition, you then stumble onto excrescences of twisted expression, flimsiness of fabric, and discontinuities.[20]

Authorship: al-Khalīl or Ibn Shuqayr?

The main point of controversy, as Qabāwa indicates, is that one of the traditional sources of information about the text, the *Tārīkh al-ʿulamāʾ al-naḥwiyyīn min al-baṣriyyīn wa l-kūfiyyīn*, by Ibn Maʿsar al-Mufaḍḍal bin Muḥammad al-Maʿarrī (d. A.H. 442/A.D. 1050), states in the biography of grammarian Abū Bakr Ibn Shuqayr, "He has a book which has been called *al-Jumal*; occasionally this book has been attributed to al-Khalīl, and they say about it: "The accusative/subjunctive has forty aspects, and the nominative/ indicative thus and such."[21] Apparently, from that time on, other biographers followed the lead of Ibn Maʿsar, and, as Qabāwa points out, "the transfer of attribution of *al-Jumal* from al-Khalīl ibn Aḥmad al-Farāhīdī to Ibn Shuqayr was [actually] done by Ibn Maʿsar alone. From him Yāqūt al-Hamawī took it, and all that followed, up to the present."[22]

An earlier author, the tenth century historian-biographer Ibn al-Nadīm (d. A.H. 380/A.D. 990), has the following brief entry on Ibn Shuqayr in his encyclopaedia, *al-Fihrist*:

> Abū Bakr ʻAbdallāh ibn Muḥammad ibn Shuqayr the grammarian. The shaykh Abū Saʻīd,[23] may Allāh be merciful upon him, said that he mixed the two schools [of al-Basrah and al-Kufah]. Among his books were: Abridgement of Grammar; The Shortened and the Lengthened; Masculine and Feminine.[24]

Thus there is no mention of a work entitled *al-Jumal fī al-naḥw* under the entry for Ibn Shuqayr in the *Fihrist*, composed about sixty years before Ibn Maʻsar's work, and certainly closer in time to the life of Ibn Shuqayr.[25]

Qabāwa points out that the copy he used as the base manuscript for his edition, states that "the accusative/subjunctive has fifty-one aspects." This copy, from the Aya Sofya Library in Istanbul, is attributed to al-Khalīl ibn Aḥmad, "and the date of the copy is [A.H.] 601 ([A.D.] 1204), transmitted from an earlier copy, and compared with it."[26]

The impression one receives, after focusing on the document as a whole for an extended period of time, is that there has been more than one hand involved in its construction, but that there is also a nucleus of analysis that is succinct and coherent. Although the text may have been elaborated upon by others since its creation, there is integrity to its core.[27]

One feature that points to its early origins and possible authorship by al-Khalīl is the paucity of references to or citations of other grammarians. Abū ʻAmr [ibn al-ʻAlāʼ] (d. A.H.154/A.D. 771) and [Naṣr ibn] ʻĀṣim (d. A.H. 89/A.D. 707) are mentioned together as authorities on the Qurʾān (p. 231). A verse of poetry is cited (p. 120) which the editor identifies as belonging to Abū l-Aswad al-Duʾalī (d. A.H. 69/A.D. 688) as well as another belonging to Abū ʿAmr (p. 203). There is one mention of al-Khalīl's contemporary, Yūnus ibn Ḥabīb (d. A.H. 182/A.D. 798) (p.61), one each of Sībawayh (p. 288) and al-Farrāʾ (d. A.H. 207/A.D. 822) (p. 156). The latter two occur at the ends of paragraphs and may be later insertions, since in view of their death dates, they may not have been considered authorities by al-Khalīl, although they were younger contemporaries. There are three references to *naḥwiyyīn*, or "grammarians," (pp. 113, 115, and 142), one to *ahl al-naḥw*, "people of grammar," (p. 63) and one to *ahl al-maʿrifa*, "people of knowledge," (p. 203).[28] That makes only twelve references in all to other language scholars besides the author.

Sībawayh, on the other hand, in his authoritative book on grammar, has hundreds (972 according to Troupeau)[29] of citations of his teachers and other language scholars, including al-Khalīl (608 times), Yūnus ibn Ḥabīb (217 times), Abū l-Khaṭṭāb (58), Abū ʿAmr [ibn al-ʿAlāʾ] (57), ʿĪsā ibn ʿUmar al-Thaqafī (20), Ibn Abī Isḥāq (7) and Hārūn (5).

Although perhaps not inscribed by al-Khalīl himself, the nature of the discourse structure (including third person references to al-Khalīl on pp. 33, 115, 134, and 181), the systematic nature of the coverage, and the scarcity of references to other language scholars, indicate that the nucleus of this text is from a very early period. It could be a compilation of notes taken by students of al-Khalīl, some of which are fairly direct reports of what was said, other parts of which are indirect, and some added later. There is a precedent for this in that the *Kitāb al-ʿayn* is widely thought to have been completed by a disciple of al-Khalīl (al-Layth ibn al-Muẓaffar ibn Naṣr ibn Sayyār) although al-Khalīl initiated the idea and most probably composed the introduction as well as the first section of the lexicon.[30]

One way to confirm or disprove its ascription to al-Khalīl would be to compare the entire body of citations regarding *iʿrāb* attributed to al-Khalīl in Sībawayh's book with the observations made in this text. Qabāwa specifies in his footnotes where the citations are mentioned in other Arabic grammars, including Sībawayh's. I have noted certain instances of congruence, but a complete investigation and comparison is beyond the scope of this project.

Sellheim, in his *Encyclopedia of Islam* entry on al-Khalīl, remarks: "It has yet to be studied how far al-Khalīl's *kitāb al-djumal fī l-naḥw* corresponds to those passages which Sībawayh associates with al-Khalīl's name." He, too, notes that one manuscript is associated with the name of Ibn Shuqayr, but also lists other copies attributed to al-Khalīl, including one in Tehran. He further remarks that "Ibn Khallikān, *Wafayāt*, Cairo, 1367/1948 ii, 17, no. 206, may well be referring to the *Kitāb al-djumal* when he mentions a *kitāb fī l-ʿawāmil* among al-Khalīl's works."[31]

Jalāl al-Dīn ʿAbd al-Raḥmān al-Suyūṭī (d. A.H. 911/A.D. 1505), lists *al-Jumal* as one of the works of al-Khalīl.[32] Moreover, the biographer ʿAlī ibn Yūsuf al-Qifṭī also attributes a *Kitāb al-ʿawāmil* ("Book of [Syntactic] Operators") to him,[33] just as Ibn Khallikān does.[34] Moreover, ʿAbdallāh Darwīsh, in his book on Arabic lexicography, *al-Maʿājim al-ʿarabiyya*, includes *al-Jumal* in his list of works by al-Khalīl.[35]

The Title

The title *al-Jumal fī al-naḥw* is given to at least four books through the fourth century A.H. (roughly, tenth century A.D.). The earliest is the one under discussion, then one by Ibn al-Sarrāj (d. A.H. 316/A.D. 928), a third by al-Zajjājī (d. A.H. 337/A.D. 948), and the fourth by Ibn Khālawayh (d. A.H. 370/A.D. 980). Moreover, the name of this and similar manuscripts have been given variously as *al-jumal*, "the totalities," *jumal al-iʿrāb*, "the totalities of desinential inflection," *wujūh al-naṣb*, "aspects of the accusative/subjunctive," *al-muḥallā*, "the embellished," *jumlat ālāt al-iʿrāb*, "the totalities of the instruments of desinential inflection," *jumlat ālāt al-ʿarab*, "the totalities of the instruments of the Arabs," *jumlat ālāt al-ṭarab*, "the totalities of instruments of perfection," *al-nuqaṭ wa l-shakl*, "pointing and voweling." [36]

Conclusion

In describing the life and works of al-Khalīl, Rudolph Sellheim states that:

> al-Khalīl had already found elements for a theory of the language. It is even possible that such a theory had already been formulated in a fragmentary way and noted down in lecture courses, in answers to questions about individual problems, and the like. But it started to take shape only thanks to the abundance of observations of individual cases, comparisons and proofs adduced by al-Khalīl, which gave the impulse to systematisation.... al-Khalīl was the real creator of this science.[37]

The originators of a disciplinary paradigm face an expressive and conceptual challenge: the delineation of a discipline in terms accessible to the audience but which also represent explicit conceptual categories particular to the nascent science.[38] For this reason in particular, *al-Jumal fī al-naḥw* is a useful illustration of the early development and elaboration of Arabic grammatical theory and its metalanguage.[39] To eliminate all doubt about the authorship of *al-Jumal* would be extremely difficult if not impossible, but for the time being I believe there is sufficient supporting evidence to go along with the attribution to al-Khalīl proposed by Qabāwa.

I include here a translation of the section dealing with the genitive, along with a commentary in the form of endnotes. I assume limited knowledge of Arabic grammar on the part of the reader and, therefore, explain Arabic technical terms as much as possible. The text has been reformatted for easier reading, and in order to clarify separations between examples and explanations.

Translation of the poetic citations would not have been possible without the help of Dr. Zeinab Taha, now at the American University in Cairo, who researched and explained to me most of these difficult passages. She also reviewed my translation of the body of the text. In addition, I owe thanks to two anonymous reviewers who alerted me to problems and inconsistencies. Since I am a linguist and not a literary scholar, my renditions of some passages may seem inelegant. Naturally, responsibility for errors, misjudgments, or any other shortcomings is mine alone.

Translations of the passages of scripture are taken from a bilingual Arabic-English version of the Qurʾān prepared by ʿAbdallāh Yūsuf ʿAlī.[40] Where the English equivalent of the scripture diverges substantially from the literal Arabic, I provide a more literal English equivalent for purposes of grammatical clarity.

Translator's additions, comments, or clarifications are in square brackets [ ], and information from Qabāwa's Arabic commentary is enclosed in braces {}.

Section 3 of *al-Jumal fī al-naḥw*: Explanation of the Aspects (*wujūh*) of the Genitive *(al-khafḍ)*

They are nine:

1. of *ʿan*, "(away) from; about" and its sisters[41]
2. of annexation
3. of proximity
4. of invariability
5. of imperative
6. of *ḥattā* if it is [functioning as a preposition meaning] "up to and including"
7. of substitution
8. of "heavy" *mundhu*, "since" [42]
9. of oath.

The markers of the genitive are three:

1. the *kasra* [-*i*]
2. the *yāʾ* [-*y* or -*ī*]
3. the *fatḥa* [-*a*].[43]

The *kasra* [is illustrated as follows]:

marar-tu bi-zayd-in.
I passed by Zayd.

The *yāʾ*:
marar-tu bi-akhī-ka.
I passed by your brother.

The *fatḥa*:

marar-tu bi-ʿuthmān-a wa ʿumar-a.
I passed by ʿUthmān and ʿUmar.

Chapter 1: The Genitive of *ʿan* and Its Sisters

[This is exemplified by] your saying:

ʿan muḥammad-in
[away] from Muḥammad
li-ʿabd-i llāh-i.
for ʿAbdallāh.

You also say:

marar-tu bi-akram-i l-rijāl-i.
I passed by the noblest of the men.

You make *akram-i l-rijāl-i*, "the noblest of the men," genitive (*takhfiḍ*) because of the affixed *bāʾ* [i.e., the preposition *bi-*, "by"]. Although it [*akram*, "the noblest,"] is of the *afʿal* pattern [and therefore diptote], nonetheless, you use *kasra* (*khafaḍ-ta-hu*) because it is the first term of an annexation structure [i.e., "the noblest of men"].[44] If you insert [the preposition] *min*, "than; from," [between the two terms of the annexation structure, thus disrupting it] you do not use *kasra* [on *akram*].[45] You say:

jiʾtu-ka bi-akram-a min zayd-in.
I have brought you [one] nobler than Zayd.

God, may He be exalted, has said in *al-Nisā'* {86}:

> *fa-ḥayy-ū bi-aḥsan-a min-hā, aw rudd-ū-hā.*
> Meet it with a greeting still more courteous, or
> (at least) of equal courtesy.[46]

He did not inflect (*lam yaṣrif*) [the word *aḥsan* "better," with *kasra*, because it is diptote]. He said {*al-Naḥl* 96 and 97}:

> *bi-aḥsan-i mā kān-ū ya'mal-ūna.*
> according to the best of their actions.[47]

He inflected *aḥsan*, "the best," [in the genitive, with -*i*] because *mā*, "what," is [in] the place of (*maḥall*) a noun, but *min*, "than, from," is a preposition --- and a preposition cannot be annexed (*lā tuḍāf-u ṣifat-un*).[48] As Dhū al-Rumma said:

> *bi-afḍal-a, fī l-barriyyat-i, min bilāl-in*
> *idhā mayyal-ta bayna-humā miyāl-an.*
> There is no man better than Bilāl in the world
> If you are comparing truly among them.[49]

He used a *fatḥa (naṣaba)* on *al-afḍal*, "the best," because of its annexation (*li-iḍāfati-hi*) to a preposition [rather than to a noun].[50] Another said {unattributed}:

> *wa mā faḥl-un bi-anjab-a min abī-kum*
> *wa mā khāl-un bi-akram-a min tamīm-i.*
> There is no man of nobler descent than your father;
> And no uncle is more generous than Tamīm.

Chapter 2: The Genitive of the Annexation Structure

[This is exemplified by] their saying:

dār-u zayd-in
the house of Zayd

or

ghulām-u ʿamr-in.
the servant boy of ʿAmr.

You make *zayd* genitive by annexing *dār*, “house,” to it.[51]

Chapter 3: The Genitive of Proximity

[This is exemplified by] their saying:

marar-tu bi-rajul-in ʿajūz-in umm-u-hu.
I passed by a man whose mother is old.[52]

and

marar-tu bi-rajul-in ṭāliq-in imraʾat-u-hu.
I passed by a man whose wife is divorced.

You make *ʿajūz*, “old,” genitive although it is not an attribute (*naʿt*) of *rajul*, “man.” Despite the fact that it is an attribute (*naʿt*) of *umm*, “mother,” you make it genitive because of closeness and proximity [to the word *rajul*.]
Likewise, you say:

marar-tu bi-mraʾat-in shaykh-in abū-hā.

I passed by a woman whose father is an old man.

You make *shaykh*, "old man; chief" genitive although it is an attribute of (*min naʿt-i*) *al-ab*, "father," [which is in the nominative case]. You make it genitive because it is adjacent to *imraʾa*, "woman, wife." He made *abū-hā*, "her father," nominative because of its being the headword [of an underlying equational sentence, i.e, "Her father is an old man."]. If you say:

> *marar-tu bi-rajul-in ṭāmith-in il-marʾat-u,*
> I passed by a man whose wife is menstruating,

it is not permitted, because *rajul*, "man," is indefinite and *al-marʾat-u* is definite, and [thus] the two items differ [in definiteness]. It is permitted to say:

> *marar-tu bi-l-rajul-i l-ṭāmith-i l-marʾat-u,*
> I passed by the man whose wife is menstruating,

because there the two expressions are equal in terms of *alif* and *lām* [the definite article].[53] You say:

> *raʾay-tu rajul-an ʿajūz-an umm-u-hu.*
> I saw a man whose mother is old.

and

> *marar-tu bi-rajul-in dhanūb-in faras-u-hu.*
> I passed by a man whose horse is thick-tailed.

If, [however,] the item in proximity is a noun, in this kind [of expression], the [case inflection by] proximity is not permitted and it

is not made genitive.
You say:

marar-tu bi-rajul-in zayd-un abū-hu.
I passed by a man whose father is Zayd.

and

marar-tu bi-rajul-in ḥadīd-un bāb-u-hu.
I passed by a man whose door is iron.

You make *zayd* [a proper name] and *ḥadīd*, "iron," nominative because of [their being, respectively] headword [of an underlying equational sentence --- *zayd-un abū-hu*, "Zayd is his father,"] and the predicate [of an underlying equational sentence, *bāb-u-hu ḥadīd-un*, "His door is iron."] You do not use the genitive [on *zayd* or *ḥadīd*] because [each of these] is a noun and not an adjective.

They used the genitive, also, as in the saying of the poet {unattributed}:

aṭūf-u, bi-hā, lā arā ghayr-a-hā
kamā ṭāf-a, bi-l-bī'at-i, l-rāhib-i.
I circle around her, seeing none but her;
As circles the monk in a church.

He made *rāhib*, "monk," genitive because of nearness and proximity [to *bī'at-i*, "church,"], although its functional slot is nominative. As they have said:

hādhā juḥr-u ḍabb-in kharib-in.
This is a damaged lizard hole.

He made *kharib*, “damaged,” genitive although it is the modifier of *juḥr*, “hole,” because of its proximity to *ḍabb*, “lizard.”[54] There is also the saying of God, may He be exalted, in *al-Burūj* {15}:

dhū l-ʿarsh-i l-majīd-i
Lord of the Throne of Glory[55]

and in *al-Dhāriyāt* {58}:

dhū l-quwwat-i l-matīn-i.
Lord of Power, --- Steadfast (for ever)[56]

He made *majīd*, “glory,” and *matīn*, “steadfast,” genitive because of closeness and proximity [to the preceding word]. It is [also] read:

dhū l-ʿarsh-i l-majīd-u
dhū l-quwwat-i l-matīn-u

using the nominative [on *majīd*,] because it is an attribute of *dhū l-ʿarsh*, “Lord of the throne.” (It is in the place of of an adjective, and an attribute [*ṣifa*] is [for reference to] God, may He be exalted. An adjective [*naʿt*], is [used] for created things).[57]

God has said, may He be splendid and strong, {*Yūsuf* 18}:

wa jāʾū, ʿalā qamīṣ-i-hi, bi-dam-in kadhib-in.
They stained his shirt with false blood.

He made *kadhib*, “false,” genitive because of [its] nearness and proximity [to *dam*, “blood”], although its underlying case is [accusative] *kadhib-an*, with the meaning:

> *wa jāʾū kadhib-an ʿalā qamīṣ-i-hi bi-dam-in.*
> They falsely stained his shirt with blood.

The poet said {unattributed}:

> *fa-yā maʿshar-a l-ʿuzzāb-i, in ḥān-a shurb-u-kum*
> *fa-lā tashrab-ū, mā ḥajj-a li-llāh-i rākib-i*
> *sharāb-an, li-ghazwān-a l-khabīth-i, fa-inna-hu*
> *yubāhit-u-kum, min-hū, bi-īmān-i kādhib-i.*
> O group of bachelors! When your drinking time comes,
> Do not drink; there is no drink for riders on pilgrimage.
> That (drink) of Ghazwān, the evil one, indeed he
> Accuses you, with it, of a liar's oath.

He made *rākib*, "rider," genitive because of proximity [to *allāh-i*, "God,"], but its underlying case is nominative because of its being the subject of the verb [*ḥajj-a*, "to go on pilgrimage"]. Likewise {Imruʾ al-Qays}:

> *ka-anna thabīr-an, fī ʿarānīn-i wadf-i-hi,*
> *kabīr-u unās-in, fī bijād-in, muzammal-i.*
> It was as though Mt. Thabīr at the start of rainfall
> Were like a huge person wrapped in a striped garment.

He made *muzammal*, "wrapped," genitive because of proximity [to *bijād*, "striped garment,"] although it is an adjective for *kabīr*, "big," and its underlying case is [therefore] nominative. Another said {unattributed}:

ka-anna-mā khālaṭ-at, quddām-a aʿyun-i-hā,
quṭn-an, bi-mustaḥṣid-i l-awtār-i, maḥlūj-i.
As though she spun, before her eyes,
Ginned cotton with a firm string.

He made *maḥlūj*, "ginned cotton," genitive, although it is the modifier of *quṭn*, "cotton."

****

As for the saying of the poet {ʿUbayd Allāh ibn Qays al-Ruqayyāt}:

kayf-a nawm-ī, ʿalā l-firāsh-i, wa lammā
tashmal-i l-shām-a ghārat-un, shaʿwāʾ-u?
tudhhil-u l-shaykh-a, ʿan banī-hi, wa tubdī
ʿan khidām-i l-ʿaqīlat-u, l-ʿadhrāʾ-u.
How can I sleep in bed, while
A devastating raid has not yet encompassed Syria
That causes an old man to forget his sons
And [in which] the virgin woman reveals anklets.

He used the nominative on *ʿaqīla*, "woman," because he intended [to put] nunation on *khidām*, "anklet." It is permissible for him to use nominative after nunation.

They may use *min*, [which is normally used as a preposition meaning "from,"] in the meaning of *kadhdhib* [*sic*],[58] "lie," having to do with *mayn*, "lie, falsehood," [in which case] it [this usage] may seem ambiguous to the hearer, as he said {unattributed}:

wa fī kutub-i l-ḥajjāj-i ansāb-u maʿshar-in
taʿallam-a-hā, min-nā yazīd-a wa mazyad-ā.

In the books of Ḥajjāj are the genealogies of tribes
Which he learned. We did not believe Yazīd and Mazyad.

where the meaning of *min-nā* is *kadhdhab-nā*, "we disbelieved." Therefore, he made *yazīd*, [a proper name] accusative [as object of the verb]. Another said {unattributed}:

inna-mā umm-a khālid-un, yawm-a jā'at
baghlat-u l-zaynabiyy-i min, qaṣr-u, zayd-ā.
Indeed, Khalid's head was injured, the day
The mule of Zaynabiyya came, so disbelieve Zayd,
O Qaṣr!

It is said that [the expression] *umm-a fulān-un*, [refers to] one's head being split open to the point where the split reaches the skull. He made *khālid* [a proper name] nominative because it is the subject of a passive verb. In his saying *min qaṣr-u, zayd-ā*[*min*] means *kadhdhib*, "disbelieve." [The word] *qaṣr* is a noun [name] in the vocative. [It is] as though he had said:

yā qaṣr-u, kadhdhib zayd-an.
O Qasr, disbelieve Zayd!

There are many [instances] like this. Get to know them so that they do not seem strange or obscure to you when they arise.

Chapter 4: The Genitive of Indeclinability

The defect of indeclinability is a property of nouns: [if] they are annexed when they are defective, and if you delete the annexation structure, they remain defective and [their] indeclinability is imposed upon them,[59] such as [the words]:

qaṭām-i (a woman's name)
darāk-i
nazāl-i
ḥadhām-i (a woman's name)
badād-i
raqāsh-i

These nouns remain in the "genitive" and without nunation [in all cases]. It is said:

atat-nī qaṭām-i.
Qatāmi reached me.
marar-tu bi-qaṭām-i.
I passed by Qatāmi.
ra'ay-tu qaṭām-i.
I saw Qatāmi.[60]

[The word] *ḥadhām-i* [also] remains in the genitive, without nunation. The poet said {Lujaym ibn Sa'b}:

idhā qāl-at ḥadhām-i fa-ṣaddiq-ū-hā
fa-inna l-qawl-a mā qāl-at ḥadhām-i.
If Ḥadhāmi says something, believe her;
Indeed the truth is what Ḥadhāmi says.

You say:

> *kaway-tu-hu waqā'-i.*
> I branded it on its haunches.
> *jā'-at-i l-khayl-u badād-i.*
> The horses came dispersed.

i.e., *mutabaddid-īna*, "dispersed, scattered." The poet said {Ḥassān ibn Thābit}:

> *kun-nā thamāniyat-an, wa kān-ū jaḥfal-an*
> *lajib-an, fa-shull-ū bi-l-rimāḥ-i, badād-i.*
> We were eight, and they were a multitude,
> A boisterous army; then they were scattered by spears.

i.e. *mutabaddid-īna*, "scattered." You use the genitive when the first part of the word has *fatḥa*, as in *nazāl-i*. [The expression] *tarāk-i* is from *al-tark*, "leaving."[61] Another [poet] said {'Awf ibn al-Ahwas}:

> *wa kun-tu idhā munī-tu, bi-khaṣm-i saw'-in*
> *dalaf-tu la-hu, fa-akwī-hi, waqā'-i.*
> Whenever I had an evil opponent,
> I used to approach him, then I would brand
> him on his haunches.

These [*waqā'-i*] are the two rounded parts on the inner haunches of a donkey.

It is said:

> *inṣabb-a 'alay-him min ṭamār-i.*

They were inundated from a high place.

which [*ṭamār-i*] is an elevated place. The poet {Sulaym ibn Sallām} said:

fa-in kun-ti lā tadr-īna mā l-mawt-u fa-nẓur-ī
ilā hāniʾ-in fī l-sūq-i, wa-bn-i ʿaqīl-i
ilā baṭal-in, qad ʿaffar-a l-sayf-u khadd-a-hu
wa ākhar-a, yahwī min ṭamār-i, qatīl-i.
If you (f.) do not know what death is, look
At Hāniʾ, in the market place, and at Ibn ʿAqīl;
At a hero whose cheek has been smeared with
dust by the sword,
And at another, falling from a high place, killed.

He said *ṭamār-i*, with *kasra*. {*ṭamār-a* is also said.}
It is said:

nazal-at ʿalā l-nās-i bawār-i.
A disaster befell the people.

He {Abū Mukʿit al-Ḥārith ibn ʿAmr} has sung:

qutil-at, fa-kān-a tabāghiy-an, wa taẓālum-an
inna l-taẓālum-a, fī l-ṣadīq-i, bawār-i.
fa-kān-a awwal-a mā athbat-a tahārash-at
awlād-u ʿurj-in, ʿind-a kull-i wijār-i.
She was killed and it was an outrage and injustice;
Indeed, injustice to a friend is a disaster.
And as soon as it was confirmed,

The hyena cubs fought in every den.

[Thus] he said *bawār-i*, "disaster," although its functional slot is nominative [as predicate of an equational sentence.]

There is a saying of ʿAmr ibn Maʿdikarib:

aṭal-tu firāṭ-a-hum, ḥattā idhā mā
qatal-tu sarāt-a-hum kān-at qaṭāṭ-i.
I gave them plenty of respite, so when I
Killed their lord, it sufficed me.

i.e., *qaṭ-ī wa ḥasb-ī*, "sufficed me."

As for the saying of another {unattributed}:

yā umm-a ʿāʾishat-a, lan turāʿī
kull-u banī-ki baṭal-in, shajāʿ-i.[62]
O mother of ʿĀʾisha! You will not be afraid;
Every son of yours is a brave hero.

Al-Khalīl has stated that the genitive on *baṭal-in shajāʿ-i*, "brave hero," was by right of pre-emption [*bi-shufʿat-i*] of the *kāf* of *banī-ki*, "your sons."[63]

[The word] *ams-i*, "yesterday," is also "genitive" (*makhfūḍ*) [even] when [it is] an agent (subject) or a direct object. You say:

atay-tu-hu ams-i.
I reached him yesterday.

dhahab-a ams-i bi-mā fī-hi.
Yesterday has gone, with whatever was in it.

kān-a ams-i yawm-an mubārak-an.
Yesterday was a blessed day.

inna ams-i yawm-un mubārak-un.
Verily, yesterday [was] a blessed day.

If you attach *alif-lām* [the definite article] to it, or you annex it to something, or you make it indefinite, then you inflect it. You say:

kān-a l-ams-u yawm-an mubārak-an.
"The" yesterday was a blessed day.

inna l-ams-a l-māḍiy-a yawm-un mubārak-un.
Verily, "the" past yesterday [was] a blessed day.

kān-a ams-u-kum yawm-an ṭayyib-an.
Your yesterday was a good day.

The poet said {unattributed}:

wa lā yudrak-u l-ams-u, l-qarīb-u, idhā maḍā
bi-marr-i quṭāmiyy-in, min-a l-ṭayr-i, ajdal-ā.
Near yesterday cannot be reached once it has passed;
[Even] by the passage of a hawk, the strongest of birds.[64]

Zuhayr said:

wa a'lam-u mā fī l-yawm-i, wa l-ams-i, qabl-a-hu

wa lākinna-nī, ʿan ʿilm-i mā fī ghad-in, ʿamī.
And I know what is in today and what [was in]
yesterday, before it.
But I, regarding knowledge of what is in tomorrow,
am blind.

inflecting it [in the genitive].

As for the saying of al-ʿAjjāj:

la-qad raʾay-tu ʿajab-an, mudh ams-ā
ʿajāʾiz-an, mithl-a l-saʿālī, khams-ā
yaʾkul-na ajmaʿ-u-hunna, hams-an, hams-ā
lā tarak-a llāh-u, la-hunna, ḍirs-ā.
I have seen strange things, since yesterday:
Old women, like female demons, five [of them]
Eating, all of them, whispering, whispering;
May God not leave a molar to them!

He made the *sīn* [of *ams*] "flexible" (*ḥarf-an layyin-an*), and changed it [i.e., its case marker] to accusative (*ṣaraf-a-hā ilā al-naṣb*).

[The expression] *ṣamām-i*, is [also] used, as {al-Aswad ibn Yaʿfur} said:

ghadar-at yahūd-u, wa aslam-at jīrān-u-hā
ṣamm-an, li-mā faʿal-at yahūd-u, ṣamām-i.
The Jews dissembled while their neighbors became Muslims;
May a calamity befall [the Jews] for what the Jews did.

He left nunation off *yahūd*, "Jews," intending it to have the definite article. Had it not been for that, he would have nunated it. Likewise is another {Imruʾ al-Qays}:

> *aṣāḥ-i, tarā burayq-an, habb-a wahn-an*
> *ka-nār-i majūs-a, tastaʿir-u istiʿār-an?*[65]
> O friend! Did you see lightening flash at midnight,
> Like the fire of the Magi, blazing bright?

He intended *alif-lām* for *majūs*, "Magi," and therefore left off the nunation.

As for their saying:

> *rajul-un bajāl-un,*
> A formidable man

if he is great and old, or

> *imraʾat-un ḥaṣān-un wa razān-un*
> a chaste and sober woman

> *imraʾat-un dharāʿ-un*
> a woman expert in spinning

i.e., *sarīʿat al-ghazl*, "a fast spinner," and

> *faras-un wasāʿ-un*
> a fast horse

> *baʿīr-un thaqāl-un,*
> a sluggish camel

i.e., *baṭī'*, "slow,"

> *rajul-un 'abām-un*
> a feeble man

i.e., *'ayiyy*, "feeble," this [kind of use] inflects with all short vowels (*fī jamī'-i l-ḥarakāt*).[66]

Chapter 5: The Genitive Imperative

[This is exemplified in] their saying:

> *samā'-i*
> Listening!
> *baṣār-i*
> Seeing!
> *naẓār-i*
> Looking!

i.e., "listen," "see," "look."[67] The poet said: {unattributed}:

> *wa muwaylik-un, zama'-a l-kilāb-i, tasubb-u-nī*
> *fa-samā'-i, astāh-a l-kilāb-i, samā'-i!*[68]
> And Muwaylik, excrescence of dogs' [legs],
> you [dare] curse me,
> Listen, you dogs' asses, listen!

i.e., [the final word, *samā'-i*, means] "listen." Another said {Ṭufayl ibn Yazīd}:

tarāk-i-hā, min ibil-in, tarāk-i-hā
a mā tarā l-mawt-a, ladā awrāk-i-hā?
Leave them, those camels, leave them.
Can you not see Death at their haunches?

i.e., [the phrase *tarāk-i-hā* means] "leave them."

Chapter Six: The Genitive with *ḥattā* Where It Means "Up to and Including" [69]

[This is exemplified by] their saying:

kallam-tu l-qawm-a ḥattā zayd-in.
I spoke to the people up to and including Zayd.

Its meaning is:

ḥattā balagh-tu ilā zayd-in, wa maʿa zayd-in.
Up to [a point where] I reached Zayd, and
[then, also] with Zayd.

God has said, may His name be exalted {*al-Qadr* 5}:

salām-un hiya, ḥattā maṭliʿ-i l-fajr-i.
Peace! This until the rise of Morn!

Its meaning is:

ilā maṭliʿ-i l-fajr-i.
up to the rise of morn

[the word] *ḥattā* is used three ways.[70] You say:

> *akal-tu l-samakat-a ḥattā ra'̉s-i-hā.*
> I ate the fish up to its head.

[or] *ḥattā ra'̉s-a-hā*, [or] *ḥattā ra'̉s-u-hā.* The accusative [on *ra'̉s*, "head," means]:

> *ḥattā akal-tu ra'̉s-a-hā.*
> I even ate the head.

The nominative [means]:

> *ḥattā baqiy-a ra'̉s-u-hā.*
> until the head remained.

The genitive [means]:

> *ḥattā waṣal-tu ilā ra'̉s-i-hā.*
> up to the point where I reached the head.

and [also]

> *akal-tu l-samakat-a maʿ-a ra'̉s-i-hā.*
> I ate the fish [along] with its head.

If you wish, you can say *ra'̉s-u-hā* because of [*ra'̉s* being a] headword [of the underlying sentence, *baqiy-a ra'̉s-u-hā*, "its head remained."] The poet {Ibn Marwān al-Naḥwī} said:

alqā l-ḥaqībat-a, kay yukhaffif-a raḥl-a-hu
wa l-zād-a, ḥattā naʿl-u-hu alqā-hā.
He threw off the traveling bag in order to lighten his saddle;
And the provisions; even his sandals, he threw them away.

[it may] also [be recited]: *ḥattā naʿl-i-hi* and *ḥattā naʿl-a-hu alqā-hā*. The accusative [on *naʿl*] means: "he even threw away his sandals," [the nominative [means]: "even his sandals were thrown away."[71] If you wish you can use the nominative because of [*naʿl*, "sandal," being] a headword [for the underlying sentence *naʿl-u-hu alqā-hā*, "His sandals, he threw them off,"] with the verb being transitive on the *hāʾ* and *alif* [of *-hā*, "them," suffixed to *alqā*] as is read [in] {*al-Nūr* 1}:

sūrat-un anzal-nā-hā.
A Sura which we have sent down.

Whoever reads:

sūrat-an anzal-nā-hā,
A Sura which we have sent down,

does so by virtue of retroaction of the verb on it [the word *sūra*]. Whoever uses the genitive [on *naʿl* in the previous example] means:

alqā l-ḥaqībat-a maʿ-a naʿl-i-hi.
He threw off the traveling bag [along] with his sandals.

[The word] *ḥattā* can sometimes mean "and." Abū Dhuʾayb said:

ḥamiy-at ʻalay-hi l-dirʻ-u, ḥattā wajh-u-hu
min ḥarr-i-hā, yawm-a l-karīhat-i, asfaʻ-u.
The chain mail became very hot, and his face,
From its heat, on the day of war, burned.

meaning:

wa wajh-u-hu min ḥarr-i-hā.
and his face, from its heat...

If you make *ḥattā* govern nouns, they inflect according to [their being] agent [i.e., subject of the verb] and direct object. Al-Farazdaq said:

fa-yā ʻajab-an, ḥattā kulayb-un tasubb-u-nī
ka-anna abā-hā nahshal-un, aw mujāshiʻ-u.
How odd it is, even the tribe of Kulayb abuses me
As if their father were Nahshal or Mujāsiʻ.[72]

Another said {Jarīr}:

fa-mā zāl-at l-qatlā tamujj-u dimāʾ-a-hā
bi-dijlat-a, ḥattā māʾ-u dijlat-a ashkal-u.
The blood of the slain still pours out
Into the Tigris, until its water reddens.

Chapter 7: The Genitive of Apposition

Like the saying of God, may He be blessed and exalted {*al-Shūrā* 52-53}:

wa inna-ka la-tahdī ilā ṣirāṭ-in mustaqīm-in, ṣirāṭ-i llāh-i.
and verily Thou dost guide (men) to the straight Way,
the Way of God.

You make *ṣirāṭ*, "way," genitive by apposition [with *mustaqīm*, "straight way."] Likewise, in *al-Baqara* {217}:

yas'al-ūna-ka 'an-i l-shahr-i l-ḥarām-i,
qitāl-in fī-hi.
They ask thee concerning fighting in
the Prohibited Month.

He made *qitāl*, "fighting," genitive because of apposition [with *al-shahr-i l-ḥarām-i*, "the prohibited month."] It is as though he had said:

yas'al-ūna-ka 'an-i l-shahr-i l-ḥarām-i,
'an qitāl-in fī-hi.
They ask thee about the Prohibited Month,
about fighting during it.[73]

Kuthayyir 'Azza has said:

wa kun-tu ka-dhī rijl-ayni: rijl-in ṣaḥīḥat-in
wa ukhrā, ramā fī-hā l-zamān-u, fa-shall-at-i.
I was like one with two legs: a healthy leg
and another, afflicted by time, and thus, lame.

He made *rijl*, "leg," genitive by apposition [with *rijlayni*, "two legs."] It is [also] recited: *rijl-un ṣaḥīḥat-un*, "a healthy leg," in the nominative because of being the headword [of an underlying sentence, *lī rijl-un ṣaḥīḥat-un*, "I have a healthy leg."]

As for the saying of the poet {al-Farazdaq}:

> *alā ḥālat-in, law anna fī l-qawm-i ḥātim-an,*
> *ʿalā jūd-i-hi, mā jād-a bi-l-māʾ-i ḥātim-i.*
> In case, had there been among the people a Ḥātim,
> Even though Ḥātim is generous, he would not have been generous with water.

He made [the name] *Ḥātim*, [at the end of the second line] genitive because he put it in apposition with the *hāʾ* [on *jūd-i-hi*.][74] Its meaning is:

> *ʿalā jūd-i ḥātim-in, mā jād-a bi-l-māʾ-i.*
> Despite Ḥātim's generosity, he would not have
> been generous with water.

Chapter 8: The Genitive of Oath

[This is] like your saying:

> *bi-llāh-i*
> By God!
> *wa-llāh-i*
> By God!
> *ta-llāh-i*
> By God![75]

[As in] {*al-Ṭūr*, 1-2}:

wa-l-ṭūr-i, wa kitāb-in masṭūr-in
By the Mount (of Revelation);
By a Decree Inscribed,

{*al-Ḍuḥā* 1-2}:

wa-l-ḍuḥā, wa-l-layl-i idhā sajā
By the Glorious Morning Light,
And by the Night when it is still,

{*al-Shams* 1}:

wa-l-shams-i, wa ḍuḥā-hā
By the Sun and his (glorious) splendour,

[and] {*al-Fajr* 1-2}:

wa-l-fajr-i, wa layāl-in ʻashr-in
By the Break of Day; By the Nights twice five.

The oath must have a complement clause, as God said, may He be splendid and strong, {*al-ʻAṣr* 1-2}:

wa-l-ʻaṣr-i, inna l-insān-a la-fī khusr-in,
illā lladhīna āman-ū
By (the Token of) Time (throught the Ages),
Verily Man is in loss, Except such as have Faith.

Its complement is *inna l-insān-a*, "verily, Man." The *alif* of *inna*, "verily," has *kasra*, [i.e., it is *inna*, not *anna*] because of the *lām* which is [prefixed to] *fī khusr-in*, "in loss." The *lām* [marks] the complement clause of the oath.

The meaning of *al-insān*, "human being, man" here is *nās*, "people in general," because the many do not distinguish themselves from the few; rather the few distinguish themselves from the many.[76] You say:

> *kharaj-a l-qawm-u illā zayd-an.*
> The people left, except for Zayd.

It is not permissible to say:

> *kharaj-a zayd-un illā l-qawm-a.*
> Zayd left, except for the people.

Therefore, the meaning of *insān* here is "people in general."

As for the oath complement which has been suppressed, [an example is] the saying of God, may He be strong and splendid, in *al-Nāzi'āt* {1-2}:

> *wa-l-nāzi'āt-i gharq-an,*
> *wa-l-nāshiṭāt-i nashṭ-an,*
> By the (Angels) who tear out (the souls of the wicked) with violence;
> By those who gently draw out (the souls of the blessed),

to His saying [in verse] {5}:

fa-l-mudabbirāt-i amr-an.
Then arrange to do (the Commands of their Lord).

The complement of the oath [clauses which began the chapter] is suppressed. [It is] as though He had said:

fa-l-mudabbirāt-i amr-an,
inna-kum la-mab'ūth-ūna.
Then arrange to do (the Commands of their Lord)
verily, you will be resurrected.

It is said: "when?" and it is said [in verse] {8}:[77]

yawm-a tarjuf-u l-rājifat-u,
One day everything that can be in commotion
will be in violent commotion,

to His saying [in verse] {10}:

yaqūl-ūna: a-innā la-mardūd-ūna fī l-ḥāfirat-i?
They say (now): "What! Shall we indeed be returned to
(our) former state?

[The word] *ḥāfira* [means] the way that you went. It is said:

raja'-a 'alā ḥāfirat-i-hi.
He returned the way he went.[78]

They are saying [in other words, in the previous verse]:

a-innā nuradd-u fī ṭarīq-i-nā lladhī
dhahab-nā fī-hi?
Shall we return the way we came?

[And then] it is said: *na ʿam*, "yes."[79] Then they said [in verse] {11}:

a idhā kun-nā ʿiẓām-an nakhirat-an?
What! --- when we shall have become rotten bones?"

And it is said: *na ʿam*, "yes."[80] [Then] they said: [in verse] {12}:

tilka idhan karrat-un khāsirat-un.
It would, in that case, be a return with loss!

The complement of *wa l-ḍuḥā* is [verse] {3}:

mā wadda ʿ-a-ka rabb-u-ka wa mā qalā.
Thy Guardian-Lord hath not forsaken thee,
nor is He displeased.

The complement of *wa l-fajr* is [verse] {14}:

inna rabb-a-ka la-bi-l-mirṣād-i.
For thy Lord is as a Guardian on a watch-tower.

The complement of *wa l-shams-i wa ḍuḥā-hā* is [verse] {9}:

qad aflaḥ-a man zakkā-hā.
Truly he succeeds who purifies it.

The complement of {*al-Burūj* 1}:

> *wa-l-samāʾ-i dhāt-i l-burūj-i,*
> By the Sky, (displaying) the Zodiacal Signs,

is [verse] {12}:

> *inna baṭsh-a rabb-i-ka la-shadīd-un.*
> Truly strong is the Grip (and Power) of thy Lord.

The complement of {*al-ʿĀdiyāt* 1}:

> *wa-l-ʿādiyāt-i ḍabḥ-an,*
> By the (Steeds) that run, with panting (breath),

is [verse] {6}:

> *inna l-insān-a li-rabb-i-hi la-kanūd-un.*
> Truly, Man is to his Lord ungrateful.

The explanation of the genitive has finished.

Notes

1. One of the anonymous referees for this article commented that the translation of the Arabic term *jumal* as "totalities" was "not very elegant." It is, however, what I have settled on as best encompassing the Arabic meaning. It is important to note here that although the word *jumla* (pl., *jumal*) is the current Arabic term for "sentence," its other traditional meanings have to do with "totality," "aggregate," "sum," or "whole." In this text, it does not refer to the concept of "sentence," but rather the concept of totality of a topic. It is used in the same manner by Sībawayh. See Gérard Troupeau, *Lexique-Index du Kitāb de Sībawayh* (Paris, 1976), 61; Rafael Talmon, Review of Versteegh, Koerner, and Niederehe (eds.) *The History of Linguistics in the Near East, ZAL* 16(1987), 138; and also Fā'iz Fāris, ed., *al-Muḥallā* (Beirut, 1987), 29: "This word (*jumal*) indicates that the compiler deals with [all] sides (*jawānib*) of his topic."

2. A standard Arabic definition of *naḥw* is found in Muḥammad al-Khaḍr Ḥusayn, *dirāsāt fī l-'arabiyya wa tārīkh-i-hā* (Damascus, 1960), 181. He states: "It is the science by which are known the endings of words: those which inflect, and those that do not. They [grammarians] delimit its discussion to the final letter (*ḥarf*) of the word, even to [one] characteristic [of it], that being desinential inflection and/or indeclinability. The aim of *naḥw*, (among grammarians) is elucidation of desinential inflection and detailed description of its rules, to the extent that some have called it 'the science of desinential inflection,' (*'ilm al-i'rāb*). In this delimitation there is a severe restriction to the field of grammatical discussion, a curtailment of scope."

3. "The survival of a case-ending system with a very low functional yield did not take place without difficulties; rather than having a semantic function and content, case forms were slot-bound and commanded by their relative position within a syntagm, as reflected by the concept of *'amal* (rection), central in the first grammatical schools," (F. Corriente, "From Old Arabic to Classical Arabic through the Pre-Islamic Koine: Some Notes on the Native Grammarians' Sources, Attitudes and Goals," *Journal of Semitic Studies* 21 [1976], 89). Some researchers believe that even the fully inflected pre-Islamic Arabic used in poetry was a *koine*, or supradialectal aesthetic register, rather than the active vernacular of everyday tribal use and that "*i'rāb*, even at the Prophet's time, was perhaps the special property of certain tribes; for the rest, it was only the prerogative of more elevated discourse --- to be more specific, probably just of the strict, metrically based poetry" (Vollers, as cited in Michael Zwettler, *The Oral Tradition of Classical Arabic Poetry* [Columbus, Ohio, 1978], 117).

4. See, for example, Janet Browne, "Botany for Gentlemen: Erasmus Darwin and the Loves of Plants," *Isis* 80 (1989),593, where she writes, "Taxonomic systems of the past are now seen to be one of the most important resources for understanding the interconnections of culture and science."

5. See Wolfgang Reuschel, *Al-Halīl ibn Aḥmad, der Lehrer Sībawayhis, als Grammatiker* (Berlin, 1959). Reuschel deduced this essentially from the body of citations found in Sībawayh which were attributable to al-Khalīl, because, until the emergence of the text under discussion, no work of al-Khalīl on Arabic grammar was thought to have survived, although his dictionary (*Kitāb al-ʻayn*) and his contributions to the analysis of Arabic metrics and prosody were well-known. For further commentary on al-Khalīl's role during the early era of Arabic grammatical theory, see R. Sellheim's entry on al-Khalīl in the *Encyclopaedia of Islam,* 2d. ed., vol. 4 (Leiden, 1978).

6. For further discussion of the characteristics of the text, see my "Morphosyntactic Analysis in *al-Jumal fi al-nahw*: Discourse Structure and Metalanguage" in *Perspectives on Arabic Linguistics IV,* eds. Ellen Broselow, Mushira Eid, and John McCarthy (Philadelphia, 1992), 263-277.

7. See Jonathan Owens, *Early Arabic Grammatical Theory* (Amsterdam, 1990), 189: "There are two striking aspects to the work which tend to set it off from the standard pedagogical grammar. The first is the extent to which it is illustrated by examples from poetry and the Qurʾān. The second feature is the plethora of grammatical functions invoked to catalogue inflectional functions."

8. The degree to which the spoken Arabic of this era (eighth century A.D.) --- whether urban or rural --- actually incorporated desinential inflection is still a topic of debate. Although the author consistently uses remarks such as "you say" and "they say" to introduce examples of usage in this text, he may be pointing out how things should have been said in correct speech, rather than how they actually occurred in informal speech. However, it may be that fully inflected forms were in use by educated members of Arabic Islamic society at this point in time.

Johan Fück remarks: "La ʻArabiya classique a conservé dans sa flexion desinentielle un trait de haute antiquité qui s'était déja perdu dans tous les autres idiomes sémitiques, a l'exception du vieux babylonien, au cours de leurs périodes de développement pré-litteraire. Combien de temps cette flexion s'est-elle conservée dans le langage vivant? cela est controverse le fait que, au moins jusqu'au IVe-Xe siècle inclus, les grammariens arabes se soient rendus chez les bedouins pour étudier leur langue, indique que la flexion externe était encore en pleine floraison a cette epoque." (Johan Fück, *Recherches sur l'histoire de la langue arabe* [Paris,1955], 3).

9. Abū ʻAbdallāh Muḥammad ibn Aḥmad ibn Yūsuf al-Khwārizmī

(d. ca. A.H. 387/A.D. 997), *Mafātīḥ al-'ulūm*, ed. G. van Vloten, reprint (Leiden, 1968), 45.

10. al-Khwārizmī, *Mafātīḥ*, 45.

11. Wolfdietrich Fischer, "The Chapter on Grammar in the *Kitāb Mafātīḥ al-'ulūm*," *Zeitschrift für Arabische Linguistik* 5 (1985), 99.

12. See *Jumal*, 172.

13. *Jumal*, 275.

14. *Jumal*, 172.

15. See, for example, Owens' analysis of the use of *khafḍ* by al-Farrāʾ. Owens, *Early Arabic*, 159.

16. Fāʾiz Fāris, *al-Muḥallā* (Beirut, 1987). I am deeply indebted to my colleague Rafael Talmon, at the University of Haifa, for obtaining a copy of the book and sending it to me.

17. Fāris, *Muḥallā*, 32.

18. Fāris, *Muḥallā*, 31-32.

19. *Jumal*, 6.

20. *Jumal*, 6-7.

Such variations are seen by some scholars constituting a manuscript matrix which has a complex integrity of its own. See S.G. Nichols, "Philology," 1-10. Also along those lines, Siegfried Wentzel reflects that "editors and critics in many areas now believe that any surviving [medieval] text expresses less a single authorial intention than that of various 'social' forces," due to the interference of scribal processes, and that the various versions of manuscripts must be approached "'holistically,' as a total unit." ("Reflections on 'New' Philology," *Speculum* 65 [1990], 1: 14).

21. *Jumal*, 9.

22. *Jumal*, 13. But this is not quite true, since at least al-Suyūṭī (1445-1505) credits al-Khalīl with a book called *al-Jumal* (see below).

23. Abū Sa'īd al-Ḥasan ibn 'Abdallāh al-Sīrafī (d. A.H. 369/A.D. 979), a distinguished judge who was also an authority on Arabic grammar.

24. Abū al-Faraj Muḥammad ibn Abī Ya'qūb Isḥāq al-Nadīm, *Kitāb al-fihrist*, "The Book of Index," ed. Riḍā-Tajaddud ibn 'Alī ibn Zayn al-'Ābidīn al-Ḥā'irī al-Māzindarānī (Beirut, 1988), 91.

25. It should be mentioned, however, that al-Nadīm does not include *al-Jumal* under his listing of books by al-Khalīl, either. See *Fihrist*, 49.

26. *Jumal*, 9. Qabāwa's fifth revised edition (1995), received immediately prior to publication of this book, contains comparisons of yet two more manuscripts of *al-Jumal*.

27. Although the stylistic variations make it more difficult to trace the original author, it is an unavoidable reflection of the practices and values of the medieval scribal profession. "Recalling that almost all manuscripts postdate the life of the author by decades or even centuries, one recognizes the manuscript matrix as a place of radical contingencies: of chronology, of anachronism, of conflicting subjects, of representation." (S. G. Nichols, "Philology in a Manuscript Culture," *Speculum* 65 [1990], 1:8).

28. Sībawayh is also cited in the *Kitāb al-ʿayn* (see Stefan Wild, *Das Kitab al-Ain und die Arabische Lexikographie* [Wiesbaden, 1965], 17); as are some other grammarians who survived al-Khalīl, e.g., Abū ʿUbayda (d. A.H. 208/A.D. 823) and al-Asmaʿī (d. A.. 213/A.D. 828).

29. Troupeau, *Lexique*, 227ff.

30. For further discussion of the *Kitāb al-ʿayn*, see John A. Haywood, *Arabic Lexicography* (Leiden, 1965) and Wild, *Das Kitab al-Ain.* For a recent translation of the introductory chapter to the *Kitāb al-ʿayn*, see Solomon I. Sara, S.J., "Al-Khalīl, the First Arab Phonologist," in *International Journal of Islamic and Arabic Studies* 8 (1991), 1:1-57.

31. *Encyclopaedia of Islam*, 2d. ed., s.v. "al-Khalīl ibn Aḥmad."

32. *wa li-l-khalīl min al-taṣānīf ghayr al-ʿayn: kitāb al-naʿam [naghm?], al-jumal, al-ʿarūḍ, al-shawāhid, al-nuqaṭ wa l-shakl, kitāb fāʾit al-ʿayn, kitāb al-īqāʿ.* Jalāl al-Dīn ʿAbd al-Raḥmān al-Suyūṭī, *Bughyat al-wuʿāt fī ṭabaqāt al-lughawiyyīn*, ed. ʿĪsā al-Bābī al-Halabī, vol. 1 (Cairo, 1964-65), 570.

33. ʿAlī ibn Yūsuf al-Qifṭī, *Inbāh al-ruwāh ʿalā anbāh al-nuḥāh*, ed. Muḥammad Abū al-Faḍl Ibrahīm, vol. 1 (Cairo, 1950), 346.

34. *wa lladhī tuḥaqqaq anna l-khalīl ṣannaf-a-hu: kitāb "al-ʿayn," fī l-lugha, mashhūr. kitāb "al-ʿarūḍ." kitāb "al-nuqaṭ wa l-shakl". kitāb "al-naghm", kitāb fī l-ʿawāmil, manḥūl ʿalay-hi.*

The technical term *ʿawāmil* (singular *ʿāmil*) refers to syntactic "operators" or regents that influence desinential inflection.

35. ʿAbdallāh Darwīsh, *al-Maʿājim al-ʿarabiyya* (Cairo, 1956), 15.

36. According to Qabāwa in his introduction, *Jumal*, 9.

37. *Encyclopaedia of Islam*, 2d. ed., s.v., "al-Khalīl ibn Aḥmad."

38. The term "paradigm" is used in its Kuhnian sense (Thomas S. Kuhn, *The Structure of Scientific Revolutions* [Chicago, 1962, 1970], and *The Essential Tension: Selected Studies in Scientific Tradition and Change* [Chicago, 1977]). This concept provides a framework for discussing the evolution of discipline-based empirical analysis. There are those who dispute its applicability to the history of linguistics (e.g., W.K. Percival,

"The Applicability of Kuhn's Paradigms to the History of Linguistics," *Language* 52 [1976], 2:285-294). But along with Koerner, I think that "the concept of 'paradigm' (or perhaps better, 'disciplinary matrix'), 'normal science,' 'revolution,' etc., proposed by Kuhn may be useful to the historian of linguistics if he does not press the argument to a point where it no longer makes sense." (E.F.K. Koerner, *Practicing Linguistic Historiography* [Amsterdam,1989], 50).

39. "It presents an abundant number of terms in desinential inflection, in morphology (*ṣarf*) and in function words (*adawāt*), some of which are completely strange and which have no echo in ancient, historical or contemporary books, and some of which carried into history evidences which became extinct, or which differed from what was known of grammar (*naḥw*) in its schools, its orientations, and its great men." (Qabāwa, Introduction, *Jumal*, 6).

40. *The Holy Qur'ān: Translation and Commentary*, ed. ʻAbdallāh Yūsuf ʻAlī (Damascus & Beirut, 1934, 1983) (A.H. 1403).

41. i.e., prepositions. The Arabic term "sisters" as used in grammatical theory refers to words that are related in form, function, and syntactic régime.

42. The word *mundhu*, "since, ago" is considered a "heavier" variant of the term *mudh*, "since." Heaviness in Arabic phonological terminology refers to the amount of articulatory energy required to pronouce the word, and *mundhu* is more complex than *mudh*. However, no chapter describing this usage is included in the body of the text. Qabāwa does not discuss its absence, but Fāris mentions that although it is listed in the chapter headings, no such chapter is found.

43. This refers to the *fatḥa* used to mark both genitive and accusative on diptotic substantives.

44. The term *khafaḍ*, "to make genitive," is used here to indicate not only the category of genitive, but specifically its designation by means of *kasra* or *kasratayn* (nunated). One anonymous referee of this paper referred to the use of *khafaḍ-ta-hu* here as "mindless" and "unworthy of al-Khalīl." Yet, as previously noted, this is consistent with al-Khwārizmī's description of his terminology.

45. The comparative and superlative "patterns" for adjectives are essentially the same (*afʻal*), except for the fact that the comparative is used in indefinite form, normally with the word *min*, "than," and the superlative is used in the definite form, with the definite article prefix, a pronoun suffix, or by virtue of being the first term of an annexation structure. The diptotic restrictions apply only in the indefinite form; when definite, the word becomes declinable using all three desinential markers.

46. The previous line reads, "When a courteous greeting is offered you," and the literal translation of the next line is: "then greet with one which is better than it, or (at least) return it."

47. Literally "according to the best of what they were doing."

48. The author here is contrasting the pronoun *mā*, "what," with the preposition *min*, "than, from." The word *mā* can function as the second term of an annexation structure because it is a form of noun, but *min* cannot, being a preposition. The author does not use the term *ḥarf jarr*, "particle of attraction," used by Sībawayh, which is the modern standard term for "preposition," but uses the term *ṣifa*, which currently means "attribute, adjective." Owens, *Early Arabic*, 141-51, maintains that *ṣifa* is characteristic usage of the Kufan school of grammar, and points out that Farrāʾ uses *ṣifa* to refer both to locative adverbs and prepositions, similar to the usage in this text. Lane notes that *ṣifa* "as a general term for an attributive word, is also applied by [Layth ibn al-Muẓaffar] and other old writers to an adverbial noun of place or time, and to a preposition." Edward William Lane, *Arabic-English Lexicon*, (1863; reprint, Cambridge: Islamic Texts Society, 1984), 1:3054.

It is use of the term *ṣifa* (among others, e.g., *khafḍ*) that causes doubt about al-Khalīl's authorship, since he is considered a prime early example of the Basran school and these are terms that predominate in Kufan usage. However, since al-Khwārizmī's chapter on grammar indicates that al-Khalīl and Sībawayh differed on certain terms of grammar (see note 9), it is not inconceivable that al-Khalīl might have used other terminological variants, such as *ṣifa* for *ḥarf jarr*.

49. I have chosen to translate the intensifying cognate accusative (*mayyalta miyālan*) here using the adverb "truly" rather than try to render this structure literally.

50. Technically, of course, despite the author's use of the term *li-iḍāfati-hi*, there is no annexation structure (*iḍāfa*) here between *bi-afḍal-a* and *min*. That is precisely why the first term does not end with *kasra*.

The term *naṣaba*, a grammatical term generally signifying "to make accusative," here signifies "to suffix a *fatḥa*," a purely phonological concept. This parallels the use of the term *khafaḍ* mentioned earlier.

51. The brevity of this chapter is remarkable in view of the fact that the annexation structure is so frequent in Arabic syntax. No examples are given of complex *iḍāfa* structures or of the definite *iḍāfa*. This lack of attention is an indication of the greater value placed at that time on rare structures than on the common ones, the latter probably being considered self-evident.

52. This is an illustration of syllepsis, irregular or unusual grammatical agreement. Literally the sentence reads: "I passed by a man old his mother," with the term "old," *'ajūz*, being genitive in agreement with "man," because of being adjacent to it, instead of agreeing in case with "mother."

53. In fact, the attachment of a possessive pronoun to a noun (e.g., her father, *abū-hā*) is one way of making a noun definite, so that the definiteness argument could apply to both examples. However, a distinction is being drawn here between definiteness achieved through the prefixing of the definite article and definiteness achieved through pronoun suffixation.

54. This is in direct contrast with the standard grammatical rule that the modifier of the first term of an annexation structure agrees with it in case, even though it is adjacent to the second term and external to the annexation structure itself.

55. In 'A. Yūsuf 'Alī, *dhū l-'arsh-i l-majīd-u.*

56. In 'A. Yūsuf 'Alī, *dhū l-quwwat-i l-matīn-u.*

57. What is between parentheses is from manuscript "Q."

58. Qabāwa footnotes this as *kadhdhab*.

59. This is an obscure point. Apparently the author is referring to nouns which end always in *kasra* and positing that this *kasra* is the fossilized remainder of a defective suffix (-*ī*) on a definite noun.

60. Qaṭām-i is a woman's name which was common in the Hijaz (see Ibn Manẓūr, *Lisān al-'arab* [Cairo, 1970], 3:123).

61. Apparently, the use of *kasra* here is part of the morphological pattern of the word, since all the items mentioned thus far have had the pattern *fa'āli*.

62. The adjective for "brave" is normally pronounced *shujā'*, with *ḍamma* as the first vowel, but it is vocalized in the text with *fatḥa*. Lane, *Lexicon* (1508), gives *shajā'* as a dialectal variant.

63. Qabāwa states that he means "by proximity to" (*al-jarr bi-l-jiwār*) the *kāf*.

64. Qabāwa gives the word *ṣaqr*, "hawk" as the equivalent for *quṭāmiyy*.

65. Qabāwa says that in the original, the word *barīq* is used instead of *burayq*. He explains that the form "*burayq*" is the diminuative used for exaggeration (*taṣghīr barq li-l-ta'ẓīm*).

66. The author seems to be disinguishing between a regularly inflected adjective of the pattern *fa'āl* and the fixed usage of the form *fa'āli*.

67. These imperative forms are verbal nouns rather than verbs, so that literally, they mean "listening," "seeing," "looking," but they are functioning as commands. It is interesting that the verbal noun pattern used for this purpose is apparently the same *fa'āli* form discussed in the previous chapter.

68. One reviewer provided the alternative reading: *wa muwaylik-un, zama'-u l-kilāb-i yasubb-u-nī.*

69. The word *ḥattā* functions in four ways: as a preposition meaning "up to (until) and including a certain point" (in time or space), where it normally takes the genitive; as a conjunction with the perfect tense, meaning "until"; as a particle meaning "even"; and as a particle that takes a subjunctive verb, usually meaning "in order that."

70. The word *lughāt* is used here (*wa "ḥattā" fīhi thalāth-u lughāt-in*). It normally refers to a dialect or vernacular usage, but it seems to function as "mode" or "way" in this context.

71. *wa l-raf'-u: ḥattā ulqiya na'l-u-hu.* Qabāwa notes that in another manuscript version (Q), the term *ulqiya* "were thrown away" is replaced by *baqiya* "they remained," which would make more sense, in light of the previous explanation of the use of the nominative.

72. That is, as though their father were of my people.

73. i.e., repeating the preposition *'an*, "about, concerning."

74. One reviewer comments: "This is an infelicitous attempt to explain away an embarrasing *iqwā'* (imperfect rhyme). Only *Ḥātim-u* yields a normal sentence."

75. The particles *wa-*, *bi-* and *ta-* are all oath markers, and take the genitive, as do prepositions.

76. This is by way of explaining the later *illā lladhīna āman-ū*, "except those who believe." The use of the singular term, "man," is meant to be generic and not to refer to a single individual.

77. This is verse 6, according to 'A. Yūsuf 'Alī.

78. This can be taken literally or figuratively. In Wehr, the definition of *ḥāfira* is "original condition, beginning" (*Dictionary*, 188), and the phrase *raja'-a ilā ḥāfirat-i-hi* is glossed as "to revert to its original state or origin."

79. But the word "yes," is not mentioned in the verse.

80. Again, the word "yes" is not mentioned.

Contributors

Irfan Shahid is Sultanate of Oman Professor of Arabic and Islamic Literature at Georgetown University, where he has developed and taught almost all the graduate courses in classical Arabic poetry and prose, the Qur'ān, modern Arabic poetry and prose, and Arab-American literature. His research interests range from Qur'ānic studies and Arabic poetry to Arab-Byzantine relations. His book, *al-'Awda ilā Shawqī,* on the Poet of Islam and Dār al-Islam appeared in 1986, and his recent publication of Parts I and II of *Byzantium and the Arabs in the Sixth Century* (1995) represents the fifth volume of his series on Arab-Byzantine relations. He is also completing the writing of a major work, *Islam and Poetry.*

Ramzi Baalbaki is Professor of Arabic and Chairman of the Department of Arabic and Near Eastern Languages at the American University of Beirut. He is also editor of *al-Abḥāth.* Author of many books, including *A Study and Edition of Ibn Duraid's Jamharat al-lugha,* his main research interests are the history of Arabic grammatical theory and Arabic lexicography.

Michael G. Carter is at the Institute of East European and Oriental Studies at the University of Oslo, Norway. His principal research interests are the history of Arabic grammatical theory and the relationship between language, religion and law in medieval Islam. Publications include a number of articles on the history of Arabic grammar and an annotated translation of al-Shirbīni's commentary on the *Ājurrūmiyya* which is designed to give both Arabists and non-Arabists a means of access to all the important features of indigenous Arabic linguistics.

Eckhard Neubauer has studied Oriental languages, Islamic culture and musicology in Frankfort, Ankara, Cairo and Beirut. He has had teaching and research experience in Turkey (Erzerum) and Iran (Isfahan, Shiraz). From 1971-1984 he collaborated with Professor Fuat Sezgin on *Geschichte des arabischen Schrifttums*. Since 1984 he has done editorial work and research in Middle Eastern music history at the Institute for the History of Arabic-Islamic Science in Frankfort.

Karin Ryding is former Chair of the Arabic Department at Georgetown University and has published two textbooks for teaching Formal Spoken Arabic. She is currently Dean of Interdisciplinary Programs and Sultan Qaboos bin Said Professor of Arabic at Georgetown University. Her research interests lie in both applied and theoretical linguistics, particularly morphology and history of language science.